ADVANCE PRAISE FOR *MOVING ON*

"This is a must-read guide for anybody going through divorce or who truly wants to inspect their life and make positive changes. I have spent the better part of a thirty-five-year career in television helping others make the hard personal decisions to activate and motivate change. In Moving On, David shows you how to change your narrative and get rid of the negative voices in your head. Just knowing that a successful, married attorney can go through a divorce, become stuck, and not give up is inspiring to help others. If you are contemplating a major life change involving a relationship, read this book first and, with David's help, learn to navigate the choppy waters ahead with ease and come out the other side happier than you have ever been before."

—J. D. ROTH, EXECUTIVE PRODUCER FOR ABC'S
EXTREME WEIGHT LOSS AND NBC'S *THE BIGGEST
LOSER*, AUTHOR OF *THE BIG FAT TRUTH*

"David's background in clinical psychology, combined with his expertise in family law, makes him the perfect go-to guy for anyone who is struggling with what to do after ending a marriage. In his book, Moving On, David compassionately delivers practical and usable advice on how to not only get through one of the most painful experiences of one's life, but actually be better off for it!"

—DEBRA MANDEL, PHD, PSYCHOLOGIST,
AND AUTHOR OF DUMP THAT CHUMP: FROM
DOORMAT TO DIVA IN ONLY NINE STEPS

"When one door closes, another opens. This book is the antidote to post-divorce bedevilment, which we know afflicts most people and includes sadness, loss, despair, and inertia. David brings wise counsel and empathy for his clients to this commonly neglected aftermath of divorce. This book will get you moving in a life-affirming direction again."

—RETIRED JUDGE ISABEL R. COHEN, LOS ANGELES
SUPERIOR COURT, FAMILY COURT DIVISION

"David Glass's Moving On provides absolutely brilliant insight into the contemporary realities of the first year post-divorce. Written by a nationally respected expert in both family law and psychology, Moving On is a must-read for anyone who is ready to turn their life around."

—MARK MOMJIAN, ESQ., FAMILY LAW ATTORNEY,
AND AUTHOR OF MOMJIAN & MOMJIAN
PENNSYLVANIA FAMILY LAW ANNOTATED

"This book fills a void so many people are struggling with. As a Certified Divorce Financial Analyst (CDFA®), I support my clients during and after divorce, and I often see the difficult 'now what?' phase set in. Moving On is the perfect playbook for facing and optimizing those next steps post-divorce. I am excited to recommend this expertly crafted book and to see the positive changes that will come from it."

—ALEX WEINBERGER, MBA, CERTIFIED FINANCIAL PLANNER®, CERTIFIED DIVORCE FINANCIAL ANALYST®

"I am so proud of David. A therapist, an attorney, and now an author. And such a mensch! What more could a mother ask for?"

—EILEEN GLASS, MSW, CLINICAL SOCIAL WORKER, AND DAVID'S MOTHER

MOVING ON

Moving On

Redesigning Your Emotional,

Financial and

Social Life After Divorce

David J. Glass, JD, PhD

LIONCREST
PUBLISHING

MOVING ON

Redesigning Your Emotional, Financial and Social Life After Divorce

ISBN   978-1-5445-1324-9 *Paperback*
       978-1-5445-1323-2 *Ebook*

*For Carol, who shines her sunlight on and
brightens every aspect of my life.*

*And for Alex, Niki, and Andrew, who continue
to teach me how to be a better parent.*

Contents

Introduction

You can't go back and change the beginning, but you can start where you are and change the ending.

—C. S. LEWIS

It's done.

The property squabbles, custody battles, and court dates that felt like they would never end are finally over.

You're divorced.

Life often feels as if it's in limbo during the divorce period, but now you've reached the light at the end of the tunnel. You have a chance to pick up the pieces and create a new life for yourself. You're ready to move on.

The question is, how do you do that? What does life

after divorce even look like? If you're like most recently divorced people, your head is swirling with questions. Where are you going to live? How is your social life going to change? How will you raise your children? Will there be enough money? When should you reenter the dating pool?

I understand. These and countless other questions hounded me as I emerged from my own divorce more than a decade ago. It was a time of uncertainty but also a time of hope. Here was my chance to push the reset button, to examine the different areas of my life, and to make them better. But where to start? To begin making sense of it all, I created a chart with six boxes, one for each pressing life question I had. Putting it on paper took the worries out of my head, allowing me to separate my concerns into categories, define them, and tackle them one at a time. A year later, I had built a stronger network of friends than I'd ever had before, committed to a better relationship with my children, and found new love with a caring, compassionate partner.

This book arose from that journey. I have a passion for helping people navigate the post-divorce period. Plenty of books have been written about the many technical, logistical, and legal questions that come up during the divorce process, but not many pick up in the aftermath of divorce. Rather than help you select a lawyer, divide your assets, or negotiate custody of your children, this book offers a series of practical, commonsense approaches for taking control of your life and embracing your second chance at happiness.

MY UNIQUE RELATIONSHIP TO DIVORCE

The processes I share in this book come from a wide range of both personal and professional experiences. First and foremost, I am a divorced father of two who dealt with all the issues described in this book firsthand. It wasn't always pretty, and I made plenty of mistakes along the way, but I got through it and have dedicated myself to helping others get through it too. In addition to having personal experience with divorce, I have focused my career on the subject, first as a therapist and then as a family law attorney for the past twenty-plus years.

When I share my story, people are often fascinated to learn how a therapist like me wound up practicing law. In this regard, my experience is somewhat unique. A childhood interest in psychology, inspired by my mother, led me to major in the subject in college. As I prepared for postgraduate work, I narrowed my focus to forensic and clinical psychology and enrolled in an unusual dual degree program that allowed me to pursue a law degree and a PhD in clinical psychology at the same time. Through this intense program, I learned to shift between—

and eventually merge—two radically different modes of thinking, one based on argument, and the other based on listening.

Upon graduating, I practiced as a clinical therapist for just under two years. However, after a summer internship late in my degree program offered me a taste of divorce law, I found myself drawn to the legal profession, where I could take a more active role in clients' lives. After some soul searching, I decided to become a lawyer.

Even in my early days as a lawyer, I found my background in psychology to be an invaluable tool. Anyone, I realized, could lead someone through the mechanical process of divorce. I wanted to partner with my clients, give them a voice in the divorce process, and help them through what is, for many, one of the worst periods in their lives. Sometimes such an involved partnership requires some coaching or cajoling, but ultimately it leads to a more satisfying client-lawyer relationship. Clients navigating divorce often find the process overwhelming, and I take great pleasure in helping them find a path forward.

IS DIVORCE THE RIGHT CALL?

While I may be a divorce lawyer, I have no interest in breaking up a marriage that could be saved. Whenever a potential client comes into my office contemplating divorce, I ask them a series of questions before agreeing to partner with them. Before you read on, I'd like to ask you these same questions so you can be sure divorce is the right call.

IS YOUR RELATIONSHIP FIFTY-FIFTY?

No one has a perfectly balanced fifty-fifty relationship, but ideally, it falls somewhere near this ratio. My first marriage, for instance, started off about fifty-fifty, but as it progressed, I began doing more of the work. It went from sixty-forty, to seventy-thirty, and then eighty-twenty. By the time things reached a ninety-ten split, I finally decided that such a dramatic imbalance—one that, through therapy, I realized I helped create (see Chapter One)—wasn't working for me.

A good relationship relies on partners bearing equal amounts of responsibility and responsiveness. You and your spouse are supposed to care about each other and what you're building together. If one of you is doing the bulk of the heavy lifting, neither of you is likely as happy as you might think.

DO YOU ENJOY SPENDING TIME WITH YOUR SPOUSE?

Do you and your current spouse share any special activities together—such as sports, hobbies, and social engagements—or do you carry out a family life where everything is separate? For instance, maybe your wife is always heading out for "girls' nights" and leaving you behind. Maybe your husband blocks you out of his exercise classes, even though you'd enjoy sharing that experience with him. Maybe you take most of your vacations separately, only going out together about once a year.

Some couples are happy to stay married but live separate lives. However, for most of us, that's a sure sign we're not happy with our spouse. If we're not doing anything to reinforce our bonds, how do we even know those bonds are still there?

DO YOU HAVE A GOOD SEX LIFE?

Everyone is going to have a different answer to this question, but as much as it might make us blush, it's an important one to ask. Are you having enough sex? Is it interesting? Is it fun, or does it feel like a chore? It's up to you to decide how much each of these questions matters, but the state of your sex life can often serve as a good barometer for the overall health of your relationship. Politics, anger, frustration—all of it comes out in your sex life.

DID YOU TRY EVERYTHING?

Have you given it your all to try and save your marriage—

counseling, an intimate vacation together, even a short break to get some perspective? Usually when I ask my prospective clients this question, I get some variation of the same response: "There's nothing to save here."

However, every once in a while, someone will look across the desk at me and say, "I don't know. I mean, we didn't really try anything."

When I hear that, I immediately send that person out of my office with a referral for a good marriage counselor. Then, a few months later, I often get an email from them thanking me for the referral and saying that it saved their marriage.

Often, relationships fail because people don't know the resources they have available to them. Perhaps they've heard of marriage counseling, but they have a negative view of what therapy is for or don't think it will help them. This often leads to impulsive decisions. When something goes wrong, rather than try to fix it, the disgruntled partner will start looking for a way out, which eventually leads them to my office. If I can help someone reconsider the path they're on and commit to working out their differences, then I've done my job—if not as a lawyer, then as a decent human being.

That said, the sad truth is that sometimes divorce is the

best option. If you've worked through these questions, and your answers continually skewed toward the negative, then you're likely better off separating and starting over.

WELCOME TO YOUR SECOND CHANCE

If you are already divorced or are committed to the process, I hope you will find this book helps you seize your second chance at happiness. In the following pages, I'm going to walk you through the first year of life after divorce, help you reexamine key areas of your life, and offer a framework for a happier, more fulfilling life. Life after divorce isn't easy. However, with the right approach and a commitment to solving—rather than perpetuating—your problems, you can emerge from this challenging period a better person.

We'll begin with the most practical considerations: assessing where you are in your life, discussing your divorce with family and friends, and designing your financial strategy. From there, we'll address questions surrounding where to live, how to create a new normal with your family, and what to consider when pursuing your new social life. Finally, now that you've had a chance to examine and redesign your personal life, you're free to reenter the dating scene, build a new relationship, and ultimately integrate your new partner into your life. In some chapters, you'll find that you're perfectly happy with the way things are, while others might need a little work.

As you move through this book, remember that problem solving is a process. With each chapter, it's up to you to examine that area of your life, decide whether it can be improved, and develop a strategy that produces the most benefits with the fewest consequences.

Your ultimate goal is to identify and create happiness in all aspects of your life—whether at work, with your children, or with a romantic partner. In the year after my divorce, as I gradually learned to let go of the things that didn't make me happy and pursue only more fulfilling relationships and experiences, I was shocked to discover how much time I had—and how much energy I had to fill it. Suddenly I was pursuing yoga and hiking and meeting all sorts of interesting people. At the same time, I was reconnecting with old friends and becoming a better advocate for what I wanted in my work. As a psychologist and divorce lawyer, I'd known that plenty of others had experienced the same things, but nevertheless, it was all new and exciting to me.

So here's to second chances. Here's to new opportunities and experiences, whether at work, with your family, or in your love life.

Here's to moving on.

CHAPTER ONE

———

Assessing Where You Are Now

Why do divorces cost so much? Because they're worth it.

—HENNY YOUNGMAN

The first step in moving on after divorce is assessing where you are today and deciding where you want to be tomorrow. Realizing that strategy and carrying it out, however, are vastly different endeavors. If you're looking for the best way to get started, here's my advice: start with yourself.

Newly divorced people rarely ask, "What did *I* do wrong?" In fact, many of my clients tend to march into my office and deliver a long list of complaints about their soon-to-be ex before they're ready to discuss anything else. As a divorce lawyer, I don't have the time or bandwidth to take the reins and ask them what *they* did wrong in the relationship. Unfortunately, most of them don't take a moment to ask themselves this question either.

I've heard judges in divorce cases sometimes say, "Mother Teresa doesn't marry Attila the Hun." In other words, a saint won't marry a killer. In almost every divorce, both parties have contributed to the dysfunction. Your spouse may have had problems, but chances are, you're not perfect either. Following that logic, if you want to move on from your divorce, it's imperative that you start with some self-reflection. Ask yourself questions like:

- What did I do wrong?
- How did I add to this?
- How could I have helped to fix it?
- What did I do to drive my ex crazy?
- What did I do that may have caused my ex to treat me poorly in return?

If you skip the self-assessment phase, you risk making the same mistakes based on the same bad behavior, and as a result, your next marriage will be far more likely to end in divorce too. No one wants that. That's why, in this chapter, we'll be discussing the many ways you can make the most out of the opportunity divorce has given you for growth and reflection.

THERAPY AND SELF-REFLECTION

Therapy is the easiest and most efficient way to move on from your divorce, and I strongly recommend it to all my clients. It's the perfect environment to dig in and begin the process of self-reflection. Think of it as a weekly chance to speak with someone who is completely neutral on the subject of your divorce. Your therapist is there to listen to you and offer advice—nothing else.

When selecting a therapist, don't worry about finding the most expensive or acclaimed person out there. Instead, look for someone you'd be comfortable meeting with once a week for the next few months, someone who can lead you through some uncomfortable conversations in a way that feels productive.

Once you've found a good fit, start with the basics and explain why you're there: you were in a bad marriage. For the first two or three sessions, feel free to share all the things your partner has done to make the relationship untenable. Go ahead: get it all out. Then, switch the conversation to yourself. With the therapist's aid, ask yourself, "What did I do or what did I draw out of this person, why did I do it, and how do I fix it?"

My first experience with therapy came when I was training to be a psychologist, though it was invaluable in the months after my own divorce as well. Decades ago as a psychology student, I was required to attend training counseling where, in addition to providing therapy to others, I would see a therapist myself every week. I found the sessions to be a tremendous opportunity to take a break from my life and talk about my practice, my personal life, or anything else I could think of. This was instrumental in helping me leave my personal life at the door whenever I entered sessions with my own clients. Further, I enjoyed the goal-oriented aspect of my sessions. Learning to recognize what I wanted to work on and how to go about doing it was the most valuable therapy experience I've ever had.

Years later, after my divorce, I relished the opportunity to talk about issues related to my divorce. During those sessions, I forced myself to take my ex-wife's perspective and consider my actions from her point of view. It wasn't always easy, but by making the effort to balance three different perspectives—my ex-wife's, my therapist's, and my own—I gained a deeper understanding of my role in the marriage and what I could have done better.

For example, from my perspective, my ex-wife worked too much and didn't do what I saw as an equal amount of parenting. To compensate, I took over an ever-increasing share of the parenting duties until I began to feel like I was Dad plus half of Mom, leaving her with only half of her own responsibility. Some of this may have been true. I'm pretty sure my ex-wife really did work too much. However, by working through these issues in therapy, I realized that my concern was merely a symptom of a deeper fundamental problem: I had been unhappy with our relationship for a while, I didn't feel like I was getting as much love as I thought I deserved, and I was projecting this issue onto my ex's handling of our children.

When we added children to the mix, it brought a great deal of love and affection to our family dynamic. I liked this feeling so much that I became more involved as a dad than I needed to be. For instance, when we would go to parties with other parents and their kids, I would keep inventing reasons to go check on my kids. All the other parents around me were content to leave their kids to go and play, but not me. I was more comfortable being a parent than being an adult in those situations, even though I was perfectly comfortable being around those other adults.

In moments like this, I was going well beyond the 50-percent line, and my ex-wife felt she couldn't compete with me. I was so hell-bent on being super dad that I wasn't leaving any room for my ex to be even an average mom. As I became more wrapped up in the children, her response was to recede further and focus on her work. It wasn't that she didn't want to be a good mother, but my overparenting left her no room to try. It took a decent amount of therapy for me to realize my fault in this breakdown.

Later, when we were divorced, my ex-wife had custody of the children a full 50 percent of the time by agreement. I was a little worried that she wouldn't be able to be a "whole parent" during her share of the time. I was wrong.

Without me in the picture, she stepped up and became a great parent. Naturally, I didn't see this change firsthand, but I saw how it affected my children's behavior. Simply put, they became less reliant on me. They stopped calling me for help with homework, to complain, or to seek advice. When I wasn't around, they had another perfectly capable parent to handle those needs, and it was clear that I didn't have to worry about them while they were with their mom. Seeing this, I learned to give up control, take a step back, and not hover over my children so much, and my daughters grew up better off for it.

The lessons I learned through therapy paid off big when my second wife, Carol, and I had our first son. These days, I don't have quite the energy I did when I was a first-time father nearly twenty years ago. I couldn't be super dad even if I wanted to, but more importantly, I don't have to. Carol is an amazing mother, so I'm careful not to take over situations with our two-year-old. For instance, if Carol is changing his diaper, I won't step in to try and help. I won't even go get him a new outfit. I've learned that one person on the job is enough, and in fact, two people often make tasks like this more difficult. There's nothing magical about the way I handle my son or change his diapers.

Changes like this may seem small, but I know how meaningful it is to Carol. Our son is my wife's first child, and she deserves the full richness of the experience. As long as I hang back and let her take the lead, everything works out well.

BACK TO BASICS

Maslow's Hierarchy of Needs is a motivational theory in psychology comprising a five-tier model of basic human needs, often depicted as hierarchical levels within a pyramid. The idea is that needs lower down in the hierarchy must be satisfied before individuals can attend to needs higher up. From the bottom of the hierarchy to the top, the needs are: physiological (i.e., food, water, sleep, shelter), safety (i.e., physical and emotional security), love and belonging (i.e., friends and intimate relationships), and esteem and self-actualization (i.e., achieving one's full potential).

Keep this hierarchy in mind as you begin the process of moving on. In the early going, taking care of yourself and learning to get some perspective on your divorce is enough. Don't rush it. For the first six months, allow yourself to take a deep breath and just *be*. Start at the bottom of the pyramid, focus on taking care of your basic needs first, and then move your way up toward other social elements, like being a parent or being a friend once you're ready.

After you have the basic stuff down and you've settled into a new routine, you can begin to expand your self-assessment. In each area of your life, you'll be able to ask yourself, "Am I happy doing this?" If you're not, is there something you could change?

At first, though, tend to the basics. Your health is arguably your top priority. Toxic relationships have a way of eating away at you, both mentally and physically, which can negatively impact your overall health. When people finally emerge from a divorce, they're often not in the best shape. If that's you, then you have a choice to make: let these lingering maladies determine your quality of life for the next five, ten, or twenty years, or use your divorce as motivation to get back into a healthy way of living.

Embracing a healthy lifestyle takes some effort, but you'll find it's worth the work because its benefits extend into every element of your life. Still, you don't have to do it all at once. First, find an exercise you like, then dial in a healthy diet, and finally, get back into the habit of regular doctor checkups. Then, take a step back and look at any drinking or recreational drugs you might use as a crutch. Bad habits often start as a result of the negativity in our lives, and they have a tendency to linger. Now is a great time to take stock of your bad habits and see what can be dropped.

By the end of my first marriage, I'd fallen out of my regular exercise habit. Because I was busy overparenting and because my ex-wife made her own fitness a much greater priority than I had mine—her gym days were nonnegotiable, while mine were flexible—I gradually let my health fall by the wayside. After my divorce, I vowed to create a new, positive habit out of exercise. I tried yoga for about a year, but even after all that, I still couldn't touch my toes. I enjoyed learning to be present and practice mindfulness, but eventually I had to admit that the physical component wasn't doing me any good. So I moved on to hiking, cycling, and Pilates and have stuck with all three of them for several years now.

WHAT'S IN YOUR TRUNK?

Exercise wasn't the only thing I'd let go. I'd let go of almost everything that was just for me. This became all too clear in one of my earliest therapy sessions when I explained how the trunk of my car was full of stuff for both the children and my ex. I had a couple of boogie boards in there for beach trips, a variety of sports gear, and "Open house" signs in case my ex ever needed me to put one out for her. (She was a realtor.)

After hearing this story, my therapist asked, "What's in your trunk for *you*?"

Talk about a wake-up call.

What I loved about this question was the implications for both my day-to-day life and my mental health. I was making neither the physical nor the mental space for my own needs. What *was* I doing for myself? Why *wasn't* I making any plans for me?

The self-assessment phase requires you to try different things and find something that makes you comfortable. I didn't have room to do that. Once I realized I could *make* room, a world of possibilities opened up. What did I want to try? Did I have the right equipment? Here was my chance to try something new.

I thought golf might be a good outlet and afford me some exercise, but after a dozen or so outings, I changed my mind. I could enjoy myself for the first nine holes, but the second nine I just didn't care. Sometimes, I'd start picking up my ball and throwing it at the hole just to add a little variety. However, while golf might not have been a good fit, I enjoyed trying something outside of my comfort zone, and I had also learned something new and met some new people, and that's where the good stuff happens. I tried yoga next and was terrible at that too, but eventually, I found things that were more my speed. The big takeaway for me was that it wasn't a tragedy when I tried something that didn't work. I simply learned from the experience and moved on to something else.

I began to make more mental space for myself as well. During my marriage, many of my friends didn't like my ex-wife, and I had become so wrapped up in my spouse's life that I began to lose track of those friendships. Now that I was divorced, I was ready to free up the mental space not only to get in touch with myself again but also to rekindle old relationships and make amends.

To my relief, I found that most of my friends were happy to hear from me and pick up where we'd left off. Though none of them wanted to see me suffer through divorce, most were happy I was taking control of my life. Time has a way of healing old wounds and presenting new opportunities. The key is to be proactive with change and maintain a positive mindset.

RECORDING YOUR ASSESSMENT

I know I told you to start slow at first, to take the recovery process step by step, but the self-assessment process has a way of gaining its own momentum. Once I'd started, I began to think of how I could improve *every* aspect of my life, such as where I wanted to live, what I liked and disliked about my job, my relationships, my health and exercise habits, and my ability to be a good parent to my children. The more I followed these thoughts, the more I realized I needed a system to keep track of it all, so I found an extra-large sheet of paper and divided it into six sections: family, social life, work, children, health, and financials. These were the parts of my life I wanted to investigate most, though I could have included as many blocks for as many areas of my life as I wanted.

I then divided each section into two halves: one side for what I was currently doing right, and the other side for what I needed to work on. After filling this information in, I folded up the paper and put it in the top drawer of my desk at work. Every week or so, I would take out the list and use it as a motivator. If I'd improved an area of my life, I would check that off, move on to the next bullet point, and begin brainstorming a solution. Then, I would generate as many different alternatives as possible, think through each one, and pick the approach that would most likely inspire action.

Eventually, though I would continue looking for ways to improve myself, I had checked off all the major needs I'd identified on my list.

If you follow a system during the self-assessment phase, you're more likely to follow through on your goals. I enjoyed looking at my list, coming up with a game plan for the week, and then breaking that plan down into daily tasks. I encourage you to get out a piece of paper and try a similar assessment. You'll see your needs more clearly when they're not swimming around in your head.

Not only does writing down your goals help you stay organized and tackle your issues a few at a time, but it can also lead to a sense of accomplishment. Whenever you discover a solution, even if just temporarily, you can cross that item off and move on to the next one. If you can, prioritize areas that need the most help most urgently. The sooner you start tackling the major issues, the easier the process becomes. Here's an example of how your goals table could look:

FAMILY LIFE	SOCIAL LIFE	CHILDREN
Do my children still enjoy family get-togethers? If so, what do they enjoy about them?	What old friends could I get reacquainted with?	How can I get my children to be neater or at least pick up after themselves?
Am I giving my children the freedom to choose to be with their friends rather than be with me?	Where could I meet some new friends? What kinds of things would we enjoy doing together?	What kinds of things would the kids enjoy that I would enjoy doing as well?
	Who could I ask for introductions for dating relationships?	

HEALTH	WORK	FINANCIAL
I need to schedule an annual physical exam.	Why have I retained my ineffective receptionist? How hard would it be to find someone better?	Where am I spending unseen money, and how can I cut that down?
What kinds of exercise could I add that I would actually enjoy (rather than just tolerate)?	Am I happy working where/ how I am, and what could I change to make it better?	Do I have extra money to spend on helpers to make my homelife more enjoyable?

CLEANING HOUSE

The more areas of your life you target for an overhaul, the more manageable you find the process, and the more you realize how interconnected the areas are. Most likely, during the last couple of years of your marriage, many parts of your life suffered. Left unchecked, the anger, depression, sadness, and general surliness you were feeling at home likely started to follow you into work, your social life, your alone time, and most every other part of your world.

This is a problem. If you can't go home and recharge, or if going home isn't a safe place or makes you feel uncomfortable, you will feel more and more depleted until you're indifferently skating through the days doing the bare minimum to be a productive human being. You won't have the energy or positive outlook to even consider addressing anything else.

After your divorce, your homelife begins to recover, and so does your energy. Feeling this sense of renewal, you can breathe a sigh of relief knowing you got out before it was too late. However, now you have a choice: take this newfound energy and reinvest it in other areas of your life, or let inertia keep you right where you are. If you don't start to make changes, you will continue to slog through your old life—plodding through your workday, coming home to an empty house half the week, and falling into the same old unhappiness trap. You always have a choice: either remain sitting in the mud puddle you find yourself in, or get on your feet and get out of it.

Remember, while sometimes it may not feel like it, divorce is your second chance at happiness. The longer you choose to stay in that mud puddle, the more likely those same problems will follow you into future relationships. If your former spouse had a habit of antagonizing you, you're more likely to put up with the same kind of treatment in the future, which will only end up dragging

THE MAN CAVE

The fun part about the self-assessment phase is that there's no one to hold you back, even when you have a silly idea. You decide what to do, what to try, and what to fix. If you make some mistakes along the way, you can go back and revisit those choices later.

When I lived on the East Coast outside Philadelphia, I had a client exiting a marriage who told me, "I can't wait to redecorate my new house. I'm going to have a giant TV in the living room, put up Philadelphia Eagles posters, and really create my own space."

I remember thinking, "All right, well, let's see how long that lasts."

I ran into him a few years later and asked how it went with the man cave living room.

"Oh, I met someone, and she made me get rid of all that stuff," he said laughing.

He had no regrets. At the time, he had the freedom to make his own decisions and try new things, and it was exciting for him. The man cave made him feel good in the moment, and even though the moment ended, he's enjoying a new moment now—living happily in a new place with a new person.

I took the opposite approach. No man caves for me. When I got out of my marriage, I didn't take any of our furniture, artwork, or other decorations. I let my ex-wife have all of it because I was already thinking ahead. "Eventually I'll meet someone new," I told myself. "She will have her own personal taste and her own furniture, and she won't want any of my stuff." So, I washed my hands of all of it.

When I rented an apartment, I rented it fully furnished and moved in with just my clothes and some books. Later, when I did meet someone, things went exactly as I predicted: we developed our own shared taste. When we bought a house, we decorated it together, largely using her existing furniture, and we didn't have to worry about some black leather bachelor sofa that I might have been hauling around.

your new partner into the mud puddle with you. You might have great intentions and be ready to embrace your second chance on a positive note, but unless you figure out how to examine and fix your problem areas, you risk falling right back into the same patterns.

CLEANING MY BUSINESS HOUSE

After the divorce, as I began cleaning house with the different elements of my life, I began looking for things in my business that drove me nuts. My information technology (IT) guy was top of the list.

No matter the problem, this guy never had a straight answer for me. He'd tell me he was working on an issue or that he'd fixed it, but then the same problem came back a week later. I finally realized I was only putting up with him because he had *always* been my IT guy. We were sitting in the proverbial mud puddle together.

One day, it dawned on me: "If I don't have to put up with my ex-wife anymore, then I definitely don't have to put up with this guy that I'm paying to supposedly help me."

I fired him the next day and hired someone new. This person came in, simplified our entire system, and most importantly, explained his process. By the time he left the office, I always knew why something happened, what he had done, and what I could do to make sure he didn't have to come in and fix the same problem next week. It was such a relief.

Empowered by this experience, next I reconsidered my billing practices. Previously, I'd used a billing service for my firm. I would dictate what I did, and they would send out my bills for me. This process saved me some time, but not enough. Even worse, it was expensive. After looking into it, I discovered that new software would enable me to do my own billing at half the cost and in half the time. I could enter my own time into the computer, my associates could do the same, and at the end of the month, I'd press a button, and all the bills would be sent out. I didn't need a billing company. I didn't need stamps. I didn't need any of that stuff.

On a roll, I started looking at every area of my business. Each day, I'd look around and say, "What do I like here, and what don't I like?" Anything I didn't like got fixed. I'd look at the problem, figure out a solution, and take action.

Every time, the process got easier, and I found it incredibly empowering. I realized that if I could get out of a fourteen-year marriage, I could get out of an IT guy from hell, an obsolete billing service, or a bad lease on a copy machine. Nothing had to be permanent. If you want to, you can change just about anything, and if you do your research, you can find a better solution. Every day, especially in the first year after your divorce, remind yourself, "I have the power to control this. I can move this forward. I can make this better."

Two years after I made these changes to my business, I had the option to renew my office lease. While I'd been accustomed to the high rents of the Beverly Hills area, the most recent hike proved too big to stomach. By this time, I was also engaged to my new wife, Carol, and, quite frankly, it drove her crazy that I didn't know how much money I would be taking in on a monthly basis. Some months, I made a ton of money, and some months, I made very little. She couldn't fathom how I could possibly be okay with such uncertainty. I understood and agreed that some stability would do us some good as we created a new life together. So I decided to move to a big firm that provided a regular draw so she and I could rely on a solid monthly number. She was happy and so was I. Not having to run my own firm anymore was a godsend. The hours I used to spend on administration were suddenly free to spend on marketing, leading to a 25 percent increase in business.

IDENTIFYING PROBLEMS AND SOLUTIONS

In my work, I meet many people facing similar decisions. One of them was a corporate attorney who had stuck it out at a huge law firm that took in twenty new attorneys every year and spit out nineteen by year seven. The others were all worked to death, had moved to a smaller firm, or quit practicing altogether. My client was the one in twenty and was now earning more than $1 million a year. She was also getting divorced.

As she navigated her divorce, it became clear how unhappy she was, and she was struggling to figure out what to do. Her firm required an enormous amount of travel and time, and even though she had become a junior partner, there were always three or four levels of people above her who could disrupt her whole calendar by saying, "I need you to stay tonight until this job is done, even if that means pulling an all-nighter." Now a single mother, she worried that she would eventually be forced to make a choice between being there for her job or being there for her children unless she found another way out.

I suggested to her, "Anything you're doing at that big firm you could be doing at a medium-sized firm. You won't make as much money, but you won't have people forcing you to put in the extra hours either, and you'll be traveling far less. In a smaller firm, you'd find it much easier to set up your schedule to work hard on days you don't have the children, and on the days you *do* have them, you can make sure you're off at five so you can be with them when you get home."

She took my advice, made the change, and was immediately happier. Sure, she took a pay cut, but by readjusting her budget and choosing a less expensive place to live, she still had more than enough money to live comfortably.

I like this story because a lot of my clients wouldn't think to make such an adjustment. If you've made it all the way to partner at a top-tier firm, how could you ever turn back from that? Simply put, if it's not making you happy, it's not worth being there. A million dollars a year doesn't matter if you come home feeling dragged through the wringer and upset all the time. What's the point of all that money if you have no time to enjoy it and share it with your family?

Sometimes, to get different results, you need to make a dramatic change. When you're brainstorming solutions to your own problems, don't restrict yourself solely to so-called sensible ideas or solutions that worked for other people. Be creative and open, and generate a pile of alternatives without analyzing them. Then, with those ideas in hand, look at each one and ask yourself, "If I did this, what would happen? What would be good and what would be bad? What would improve, and what are the downsides?"

As you go through this process, most likely one or two of your brainstorms will stand out as the best choices to make even if they seemed crazy at first. If you can identify one clear winner, that makes it even easier. If there are two, you have to examine them a little more closely, but eventually, one solution or the other will emerge as the obvious best choice.

RELATIVE STABILITY VS. HAPPINESS

All of our decisions require us to make choices between relative stability and happiness. Relative stability is something most of us are familiar with. Think of it as the way we're used to doing things. This is who I'm married to, this is how we spend money, and these are my friends. There is stability in that, even if you're not truly happy, and that status quo will continue unless you make a change. Sometimes, however, you have to ask yourself whether this stasis brings happiness or whether you're just relying on that stability because it's easier than uprooting your life.

Now that you're divorced, the life that you once knew has already been uprooted. You might as well make the most of it. Take a look at every aspect of your life and ask yourself: Are you just doing things because that's how you've always done them even if it's something you hate to do? Or is there a different way you could do things that could make you happy and feel good? If you aren't pushing for happiness in all aspects of your life, you're missing out.

That said, change is always difficult. It takes a lot of energy to give your life a full audit. However, once you start making a few new decisions, each subsequent change gets a little bit easier. Soon, you might even begin to enjoy finding the little annoyances in your life and replacing them with new things that feel good.

CHAPTER TWO

Telling Your Family and Friends

Divorce isn't such a tragedy. A tragedy is staying in an unhappy marriage, teaching your children the wrong things about love. Nobody ever died of divorce.

—JENNIFER WEINER

Once you've decided to get a divorce, a series of important conversations await. Many people are afraid of telling their parents, siblings, and friends about their divorce because they have to admit failure. It's common to want to retreat from that feeling—or even to hide it—but remember that loved ones are typically supportive.

On top of everything else in this trying time, you have to admit you made a mistake. You chose the wrong partner. Or you didn't conduct yourself responsibly. Or you simply grew apart. Once, you and your partner had a plan for your family, and you were sure you had a bright future together. Now, that plan is finished.

Just admitting that you've made a mistake is hard for a lot of people. It was certainly hard for me. At the time of my divorce, I had over a decade of experience on the topic both as a psychologist and a divorce attorney. Even with all my knowledge and familiarity with the subject, I still found it one of the most difficult experiences of my life.

As I braced to tell the people I loved the truth—that our marriage hadn't worked and I had to move on—I told myself the same thing I'd told countless others over the years. Admitting failure was terrifying, but that fear goes away quickly when you realize how supportive your friends and family are. Most of them step up, listen attentively, and support you in your decisions. Some, you will find, are not as supportive. That's okay too. If nothing else, you've just taken a huge step in figuring who you will choose to spend your time with down the road.

Once you've shared the news with your loved ones, you learn that your fear around the moment is often misplaced or irrational. Anxiety is all about having irrational, counterfactual fear. There are definitely things in life to be fearful of, like crossing the street and getting hit by a bus. If you're in the African jungle, you'll probably be wary of being chased down by a lion eager to eat you. However, most of the things we are scared about exist only in our heads. Once you make the choice to move ahead, the fear and anxiety fall away (and it's incredibly satisfying to get rid of all that stuff).

As much as it might feel like the opposite, keep in mind that divorce is not that big a deal. Over 50 percent of marriages end in divorce, so most of us are right in the middle of that bell curve. There's nothing wrong with that. You may feel like a failure, but think of all the people you know who remain married when they probably shouldn't. You don't want to be an unhappily married person carrying on just because you exchanged vows and promised to be together. It doesn't make sense to be with someone who is not making you happy.

HOW TO BREAK THE NEWS

When the time comes to tell people about your divorce, it can be helpful to do some planning. Just like you did in the last chapter, it's time to make another list. On this one, write down the top people in your life, the people closest to you, the people you confide in. If you're like me, this won't be everybody. I have plenty of friends I enjoy spending time with, but I don't share the personal details of my life with them all. We'll hang out, talk about positive things, go to a game, and maybe get a drink after, but

I won't tell them what's wrong in my life because that's not the kind of relationship I have with them.

Most of us can think of four or five people we are wholly comfortable with, whether they're siblings, parents, cousins, or close friends. These are the people most likely to be positive about your new reality, and that's exactly what you need in the early going. We all need someone in our lives who will say, "I'm sorry your marriage didn't work out, but I know you'll land on your feet. I'm here for you anytime you want to talk about it. If you want to cry or scream or whatever, I'm here for you." Your job with this list is to identify those people.

Next, you'll want to reach out to them. The sooner, the better. Most likely, your divorce cost you your best confidant—your spouse. This was likely the person you went to with all your issues. Anything that went on at work, you could come home and vent about to your spouse, who was always there to bounce ideas off of, to problem-solve with, and to figure out which way to go.

Now, that person's gone. But remember, no one stands alone. Everyone has to talk to somebody. If you're having trouble making a list of candidates or aren't ready to open up to your loved ones, then share with your therapist. Bottling the complicated emotions that rise up from divorce isn't good for anybody.

Most anxiety and depression stems from the feelings we bottle up. All those thoughts and feelings you have related to your divorce, they need somewhere to go. The more you leave them spinning around in your head, the worse you're going to feel. It's important to find someone you can share with, especially people who can help you get some perspective. These are the folks who will say, "Why are you even worried about that? That's not a big deal. I know it feels like crap right now, and it will for a while, but I promise you it will get better. You'll look back on this time and be so glad you're moving on in your life." And they'll be right.

SPREAD THE LOVE

It's rare to find just one person with the bandwidth, ability, time, and patience to listen to all of your angst about your divorce. If you can call on more than one person, you can split up the burden so no one gets burned out and starts avoiding your calls. A small, tight-knit circle of people you can lean on works out much better than a single source of support.

By spreading the love, you will also find different people are good at different things. For instance, some people are compassionate listeners. They will listen to every-thing you have to say, tell you everything will all be all right, and not try to solve your problems. Others will listen and then offer advice. Sometimes that advice is good, and other times it isn't, but at least they're listening up front before putting in their two cents (though some don't even do that). Whatever the case, if you are able to talk to a variety of supporters, you will have a better chance of keeping a well-rounded and available support group to help you through a time when sound thinking and cognition won't exactly be your strong suits.

MUTE THE UNHELPFUL VOICES

Making a list also helps you eliminate people who won't be helpful. Not everyone in your circle is going to give you the best advice. Some will want to be helpful, but rather than say anything of value, they default to unhelpful I-told-you-sos, saying things like, "I can't believe you made it that long," or "I knew that marriage was a mistake from the beginning." If you've decided to get divorced, you've likely already had these thoughts and spent enough time beating yourself up over some of the choices you made. You probably don't need any outside, uninformed opinions.

Luckily, in the natural progression of things, the people who give you bad advice usually fade from your day-to-day experience. You'll stop seeking out their advice, and they'll stop looking for excuses to offer it.

None of my confidants were overly negative or unhelpful immediately after my divorce. However, after I'd spent the year in therapy getting my act together, and had met the woman who would later become my wife, I remember calling my best friend to tell him the news. He was my college roommate, and we'd been friends forever. I expected a hearty congratulations from him. However, rather than telling me he was excited for me, he said, "I think it's too soon for you to be getting involved with someone." His advice had nothing to do with the person I'd met but rather with the idea of dating overall. I was surprised at his negativity, and for a while, I didn't talk to him as much. I didn't need that voice in my life, at least for the time being.

After Carol and I got engaged, I called him back, and he asked why we hadn't been talking. I was honest. "You were really negative," I said. "I felt like I found the person that I loved and wanted to spend the rest of my life with, and you threw all sorts of shade on it, and I didn't need it then. I'm sorry we haven't talked as much, but I still want to be friends."

After that conversation, we reestablished our friendship and are now as close as we've ever been.

It might sound callous to say, but you have to find people who can give you what you need right now. After all, you've got a lot going on: you're getting divorced, you're in need, and you're at a low point in your life. You don't have the energy or patience to deal with negative people. Figure out who your supporters are, rely on them to get you through, and then figure out what you want to do. Approaching your relationships in this way will help give you a sense of control in your life when you don't have much.

LET TECHNOLOGY WORK IN YOUR FAVOR

I took advantage of technology to start the divorce conversation with family and friends. First, I drafted an email to send out to the members of my top-five list, which included my parents and a few good friends. Here's what I said:

> I'm getting divorced. I've realized that it won't work out with [my ex-wife]. I'm not happy, and by not being happy, I'm not doing the best for myself or my children. I want to fix a lot of things in my life, and it is going to take time. I'm pretty sure that [my ex-wife] and I will mediate our case relatively quickly. This is what I need from you: I need you to be supportive, I need you to be someone I can bounce ideas off of, I need you when I call and I'm upset about something to just to be there and listen and tell me it will be fine.

Here's what I don't need. I don't need you to hate my soon-to-be ex-wife. I don't need you to tell me the things that she did wrong or how you knew all along that she wasn't good.

Then, I personalized each message and told the recipient what I needed from them specifically. For my parents, I also added the following: "All of a sudden, I've got half of the assets I used to have. A lot of cash is being moved around in different ways, and I may need to borrow some money." I was up front with this need so they knew what to expect.

For a friend who lived in town, I added, "I'll now have half the time where I don't have my children, and I don't want to just sit at home alone. I need to find some things to do, and I'd like to do some of those things with you. I'll need you to go on hikes or just meet up."

Finally, I concluded by asking the people on my list to call me out if I needed it. "If I'm not making sense or if I'm talking irrationally, I need you to tell me." Sometimes you get off track, you're upset, sad, or anxious. Whatever it is, you're not thinking as clearly as you normally would, and you may need someone to bump you back on track. We all try to be our best selves at work and in our lives, but everyone needs others to rein us back in when we start acting irrationally and need to regroup.

On the surface, such an approach might seem bossy. After all, I was telling all these people how I wanted them to act. However, the way I saw it, I was simply giving them a formula for how they could be the most supportive to me that would feel good to me and that would deepen our relationship. Later, they all told me that they were grateful for the guidance. Everyone who received the email said something to the effect of, "That message was so great. I kept that email and referenced it before we would talk to remind myself what I should or shouldn't talk about."

Remember, for many of your confidants, this will be their first time being in a supportive role like this. Offering them a road map for how to best support you as an effective friend and confidant will help all of you get through the struggle and learn to move on.

WHAT IF MY FAMILY DISAPPROVES?

I have clients who say, "Oh my God, I can't talk to my parents because they're religious, they don't believe in divorce, and no one has been divorced on either side of my family going back four generations." They're convinced that parents or friends won't understand or, worse, will ostracize them.

For these clients, I advise them to add a little extra language to their email so they can address any religious, familial, or personal concerns right up front, something like, "I understand that religion is important to you, and I understand that you have beliefs that people should work on their relationships as much as possible and not to leave relationships, but that isn't going to work for me. I don't need to hear any disapproval or that I won't be accepted."

If those people can't listen to what you need from them and they insist on telling you what you don't need to hear, you have to stand up for yourself. This can be difficult and sad, because now in addition to losing a spouse, maybe you're also losing a family member (at least for the time being). However, if that family member is just going to fill your head with all sorts of negative thoughts, then they're not serving their function.

That said, most likely, you will be surprised by the amount of support you receive—even from loved ones with strict beliefs. Most parents want their children to be happy, and after they hear your explanation, they're most likely to agree with your decision to move on.

If you're certain that your parents or other trusted loved ones won't be supportive, if you're certain that sharing information about your divorce will create turmoil, it's best to keep the conversation muted for the time being. These are not the kinds of people you want on your top-five list, though do what you can to keep the door open for future conversations. Later, once they see how much happier and satisfied you are with your life, they will want to be around you to help.

GET THE TIMING RIGHT

Timing is a critical and delicate aspect of sharing divorce details. Early on, don't tell too many people. Don't even tell the people close to you until you're absolutely sure. You don't want to lay this all on them and have to back-pedal if you decide to stay with your spouse. It can create unintended crises in your relationships with others. For instance, if a friend greets the news of your divorce with an enthusiastic "Finally!" and then you and your spouse decide to try and work things out, that friendship is now strained. Wait until you are completely ready before telling anyone. Remember as well that, once news gets out, it travels quickly. Make sure the most important people know first. You wouldn't want your children to find out about your divorce from anyone other than you.

Learn from my mistake. Back when my ex-wife and I had decided to separate, I had sent out my email and told the key people in my life, but we had not told our daughters yet. It was the beginning of September, they were back to school, and we just wanted them to get a month of school under their belts before they had to start dealing with the stress of our divorce. Looking back now, that sort of faking it for a month probably didn't serve anyone's needs, but at the time, we thought it was a good idea.

One night around this time, I was on Facebook and thought, "At some point I should change my status from married to single," so I did. Unfortunately, I hadn't realized that once you change your status, unless you have your privacy settings correctly set up, that change is broadcast to everyone on your friends list. That night, my entire network learned that David Glass was now single. When I woke up the next morning, I had a pile of messages from people saying they couldn't believe it, asking what happened, and telling me how sorry they were. I was encouraged by the support, but I wasn't ready to share my divorce with the world yet. I quickly changed my relationship status back and told everyone it was some kind of computer glitch (though I doubt many people believed it).

Somehow, I got lucky with this mishap, and news of our divorce never reached my kids. Neither was on Facebook or social media at the time, and apparently, no one who was ever brought it up to them. It would have been tragic if they would have found out this way, and we were grateful to be able to share the news on our terms a month later.

Be careful with social media, especially when it comes to the status of your personal relationships.

WHAT'S THE BEST WAY TO TELL YOUR CHILDREN?

Don't tell your children until you have a plan. It's as simple as that. If you're still fumbling about emotionally and trying to get things in some semblance of order, keep it to yourself. It's too scary for children to suddenly hear, "We're getting a divorce. While we have no idea what this will look like, we'll tell you as it goes along." Children need to be reassured of how things will go and changes to come. Even more than adults, children like having a road map of what to expect so they can cross things off lists.

If at all possible, you should tell your children with your soon-to-be ex. It's much more powerful and less upsetting to children to hear it from both parents at the same time. This is bad news for children to hear, but easier on them if they see both their parents are on the same page. Write out your script and study it to be familiar with what you're going to say. Say something like, "It's going to be tough for a while, but in the end we'll all be happier. And we're going to try to keep things in your life exactly the same as much as possible." Remind them that they'll still have the same friends and activities and that their lives won't turn upside down.

If you plan on having a set schedule with the children being at mom's house certain days and at dad's on other days, explain this to them, be sure they understand how it works, and emphasize the upsides. If you tell them what to expect, what's going to change, and more importantly, what *isn't* going to change, most children end up being all right with it. The important thing is that after you're done talking, be ready to accept whatever emotion your children have, in whatever form it is, in a nonjudgmental way. Some children get angry, some get sad, and some get nervous.

My girls were nine and seven at the time of my divorce. Our nine-year-old was the serious, more anxious child, while our seven-year-old was the happy-go-lucky type. When we sat down with them and told them the news, the younger one listened, listened, listened, and then started laughing. It was a real strange, forced laughter that eventually turned into crying. We let her go through the full process and accepted her reaction. Whether they're silly, angry, sad, it doesn't matter. That's their emotional response, and you have to be there to tell them everything's going to be fine.

Ultimately, it's critical to do what's best for your children, and having both parents in the same room shows that you don't hate each other and that you will always be their parents. You're just not going to live in the same house. Doing this together also prevents any inevitable feelings of resentment toward one parent or the other. To a child, it may seem cruel to hear the news from only one parent while the other is absent.

Remember as well that children don't need *all* the information, especially younger children. The younger the children, the simpler the story needs to be. They don't need to know the exact reasons for your divorce. If they ask, try to explain that you love each other but don't enjoy being together and living together. Many children will ask why you don't get along and why you aren't doing X, Y, or Z to help. Explain that it's adult business, that it's nothing they can fix, and that it's not their fault.

In their minds, they're trying to figure out why their world is changing and what you can do to fix it. I remember giving my daughters the example that their mom and I didn't do much together, that their mom and I went to the gym and hung out with friends separately. Our older daughter said, "Well why don't you just start going to the gym together?" They only wanted to help keep us together.

We had to explain it was an adult problem and not to worry, and most children are relieved to hear that. They're confident and fall back into their routine of homework, friends, and food.

NEXT STEPS: MAKE A FINANCIAL PLAN

Once you've shared the news of your divorce with the people who matter to you most—family, close friends, and your children—it's time to start considering the practical aspects of your new life. Like it or not, money is a huge part of our lives, and perhaps unsurprisingly, it presents many challenges in divorce. You need to know how much is coming in, how much is available to spend, and how much you will have to send the other party. In addition, you will have to decide whether you're selling the house or whether you or your ex-spouse will be staying. If you're leaving or selling the house, now is the time to decide on a new place to live—just be careful that you're not living outside of your means.

A good understanding of your financial situation will help you plan every aspect of your new life: the social activities you want to participate in, the area in which you want to live, and even how often you'll visit the children. To learn how this all plays out, follow me to the next chapter.

CHAPTER THREE

Designing Your Financial Strategy

Money is not the most important thing. Love is. Fortunately, I love money.

—JACKIE MASON

Divorce significantly changes both partners' financial scenarios. This might include paying monthly spousal or child support, or returning to the workforce after an extended time away. Whichever scenario applies to you, it is important for both parties to trim budgets as much as possible and streamline support payments and career strategies.

While we won't be going too far into the legal nuances of money as it pertains to divorce, here are the basics: one party will be paying money to the other party. Always,

always, always, the person paying money thinks the amount is too high, and the person receiving it thinks it's too low.

In reality, they're both right. When you look at the big picture, you can see why. As a couple, you used to have a specific amount of money in the bank, one house to pay for, and one set of expenses. When you divorce, you split that same amount of money up, but everything is duplicated—two homes means double the expenses. There's simply not as much money to go around.

Though it may not always feel like it, the divorce code in your state is designed for each party to live at the same marital standard they enjoyed during the divorce. Unfortunately, because of those new, redundant expenses, that's impossible to pull off. You can get close, but you'll never get all the way there. As a result, you're almost certain to begin this new chapter of your life with money worries.

TRADITIONAL FINANCIAL SUPPORT SCENARIOS

During divorce proceedings, you will have to discuss both spousal support and, potentially, child support. Almost every state has a different formula for who has to pay support to whom and how much gets paid. Most boil down to what the higher earner makes on a monthly basis, gross or net. If you are the higher earner, your payment amount will be about one-third of the difference between your two incomes. Why one-third? Simply put, one-third of the difference will be paid to taxes, a third will go to you, and the final third will go to your ex-spouse.

In 99 percent of cases, this formula is the most efficient way to even out the money between parties. Generally speaking, my advice is that you take whatever the divorce attorneys figure you need to pay or receive, get familiar with that number, and start planning for tomorrow. Whether you're making the payments or receiving them, your job is to determine what you have to work with each month.

THE HIGHER EARNER'S NEW FINANCIAL WORLD

When people hear those numbers, they're often surprised, and sometimes appalled. Especially the higher-earning party. I can usually talk them down from their initial panic. At first, they can't believe they have to pay one-third of their income every month. The number always seems extra-large on paper. When they balk, I ask them to think back on how much of their paycheck went to expenses related to their partner or their family. Usually, it's nearly all of it. Then, I explain that now they will only pay 33 percent of those expenses, so they're actually saving money and have more control over it. It's not as bad as it looks at first.

Once they have accepted the numbers, I encourage them to set up automatic support payments. That way, they don't have to think about that expense every month. Payments are made on time, and the receiving party enjoys the same peace of mind. Of course, it is important to remember to balance payment dates. Rent or mortgage will always be there, so be sure support payments fall at a strategic time each month. In the end, automatic payments help relieve some of the stress of the situation, and that is always welcome.

THE LOWER EARNER'S NEW FINANCIAL WORLD

If you are the lower income earner, you face a different sort of surprise: the money received from support will not be adequate to cover everything you used to pay for or became accustomed to. In that regard, most states' family codes encourage those receiving support to return to the workforce if they have not already.

In addition to monthly financial support, the lower earner receives half of the other party's assets. Many make the mistake of relying on that. Let's say you split a bank account, and your portion is $40,000. If you start using that money to make up the difference between expenses and monthly support, it'll be gone in a few months, which sets you up for a big problem.

If you look closely at all expenses and create a budget, those expenses will likely exceed what you have coming in. First, you'll have to decide what to cut and what to keep. Then, you'll have to decide how to supplement your income.

CREATE A BUDGET TODAY TO SAVE TOMORROW

Parties on both sides of a divorce need to create budgets. Since many couples don't keep budgets when they're married, this task might be something they are unfamiliar with. Most married couples spend and save in a somewhat unstructured manner. When money comes in, they spend some of it and save some of it, and everything generally works out at the end of the year. After a divorce, when there's suddenly not enough money to go around, you have to look carefully at all expenses.

Most home bookkeeping software, like Quicken, offers customizable forms to guide you through the budgeting process. Look at whatever account you use to pay expenses and determine how much you spent and how you spent it. Then, start deciding which of those expenses you need and which you can do without. Start by comparing money coming in to fixed costs such as rent or mortgage, groceries, and car payments, to determine your needs. Then, look for ways to trim the budget to meet your goals. Most people's budgets will reveal glaring expenses that can be slashed or eliminated altogether. If, after trimming, you're still short, it's time to think of ways to supplement your income.

DITCH THE FINANCIAL BALLAST

Unfortunately, you will probably have to start with the fun stuff. Lifestyle pleasantry expenses add up fast. Those Starbucks coffee runs, going out to lunch on workdays, and deluxe cable TV packages make for a big outflow of cash every year. Start with expenses like that when you're looking to slash your budget.

After my divorce, I analyzed my spending and realized I was paying $280 every month on my cable bill. What the hell? There was always enough money, and my bills were set to auto pay, so I didn't pay attention to the cost. I rarely watch TV, and the programs my children watched were generally free or low cost. Once I considered this, I asked myself why on earth I was paying that much. After learning more about cutting ties with cable TV, I realized I could get a digital antenna to receive network channels and an Apple TV to get Netflix and things like that. After the initial cost of the equipment, I ended up paying $24 a month instead of nearly $300.

As another example, I always used to stop for coffee on the way to work—and sometimes in the afternoon too—as an excuse to get out of the office. As I result, I was spending $6 a day for 220 workdays a year. I could easily reduce that $1,320 annual expense if I just drank the free coffee at the office or brewed my own pots more regularly at home. Once I saw that large number, I decided I didn't need those fancy coffees to jolt myself awake every day.

It used to be much more work (and more painful) to pay for things. A bill would show up in the mail, and you'd handwrite a check, put it in an envelope, apply a stamp, and mail it off. You had a visual reminder of what you spent, which you reinforced by manually balancing your checkbook. However, with modern commerce so geared toward card and digital payments, you rarely see money physically leaving your hands anymore. As a result, the cost of all those comfort items you allow yourself doesn't seem real. Until you look at a budget, you have no idea where your money is going.

Automatic payments certainly have their value. Earlier in this chapter, for instance, I recommended making automatic support payments to your ex-spouse. However, when it comes to paying your bills, I recommend the opposite. The more you force yourself to actively pay your bills every month, the more aware you'll be of how much you're spending and where that money is going.

PREPARE FOR NEW EXPENSES

If, when you were married, your spouse did the laundry and you don't know how to do laundry, then you may need to find someone to do the laundry. Or you may need to find a place you can take your laundry where they clean, fluff, fold, and return it to you. If you used to clean your own house but weren't especially good at it, maybe you want to get a housekeeper so you don't spend your entire Saturday cleaning.

Considerations like these may be new expenses, but they may also be worthwhile. To be sure, simply ask yourself which cost you prefer: the financial cost of paying someone else to do the work, or the time cost of doing work you despise? Naturally, you don't want to pay for so many services that you end up with plenty of free time but no money to spend.

When I moved into an apartment after my divorce, I knew I needed a cleaning person. In my single days as a young graduate, my apartment was a pit. It was truly awful. I wasn't good at cleaning and didn't put any effort into it. On top of that, I hadn't done a single load of laundry the entire time I was married. I knew I needed a housekeeper to take care of these things for me.

In the early years of my first marriage, we used to clean our own house, and we'd spend half a Saturday getting it all done. "All right, you go do the bathroom, and I'll do the kitchen." It didn't matter who did what task. We hated all of it. We asked around and found out we could get a housecleaner for $50 a day. Since we were both working as attorneys and making plenty of money, we immediately hired someone.

After divorce, you might have more time, and if you want to give it a try, that's great. However, if you weren't doing those activities before, do you *really* want to take on more responsibilities right as you're starting a new life?

Often you won't, but sometimes you might. I had a client in his early seventies going through a divorce. I remained friends with him after the divorce, and one day he had me over to his new apartment. As he showed me around, he told me how much he loved doing dishes. He never used a dishwasher. He loved the fact that after dinner, he could take all the dishes, pile them on one side of the sink, and work through them. He was half embarrassed and half proud about it. I thought it was great. Doing dishes had not been part of his daily life in the past, and he came from a generation where the wives traditionally did that chore. However, he was happy to buck tradition and discover something new about himself.

TIPS FOR REENTERING THE WORKFORCE

If it has been a while since you've been in the workforce, you are in for a shock. In the old days, people used to scan the classifieds, circle ads, call for appointments, and mail in a printed résumé. That's not how it works anymore. It's much more likely you'll apply for jobs through an employer's website or an online job board and send your résumé electronically.

Writing a résumé is stressful even in the best circumstances. If you haven't even done that in a while, the added pressure of learning rules of the new job market can be daunting. How do you set up a winning profile on LinkedIn? How to you phrase your application materials so you don't tip off your age or time away from work to potential employers?

For these reasons, I suggest you invest in a vocational counselor. It's the smartest use of your money after a divorce. These specialized counselors help you return to work or update your skills. After a few hours of running you through basic psychological and skills tests, the counselor will compose a report identifying what you need to do to get a job. The counselor will then walk you through the report, mapping out key information such as necessary training, timeline, and earnings outlooks for a given career path. They can also offer guidance on creating résumés, identify specific tasks to complete, and suggest a list of potential jobs or companies.

Counselors are exceptional resources for those who have been absent from the workforce for an extended period of time but who are ready to jumpstart the process. Often, many of us aren't sure what we want to do, what would make us happy, or even what would earn us a respectable salary. Vocational counselors help remove the guesswork and move you along toward what's important: finding a job.

Not only will this process allow you to maximize your income in your new life, but it also benefits both parties to the divorce. If you're the party paying support and the person on the receiving end doesn't want to get a job, the court can order them to attend vocational education. If the evaluation finds they could earn more, it will likely lower your support obligation. Ultimately, the better their earning potential, the lower your support obligation will be.

Whatever the case, vocational counseling is money well spent and an effective tool to lessen the burden and foster a positive forward direction.

AVOID STOPGAP JOBS

If you have a career aspiration, taking a low-paying, temporary job isn't the answer. It may fill a gap, but it won't move you down the road. In fact, if you stick with a short-term fix long enough, it often becomes your new normal, and you end up settling for average.

Instead, think about what you want to do, seek out training or retraining, and get on the path toward your goal as quickly as possible. Take several months to attend a new computer course, for example, or find classes to recertify in a previous field. In most cases, there will be an expense with training or school, but keep the future in mind. With the right job, there's more money to be made in the long run.

WHAT NEXT?

Once you have a budget in place and a handle on what kind of money will be available, you can decide where to live. You have to have a home to provide a base of security, safety, shelter, and food. Obviously, you can't choose a place to live until you know how much you have to spend, and many people jump too quickly into the deep end and choose an apartment or home that is beyond their means. In the next chapter, we'll discuss how to make the best possible decisions when selecting your first post-divorce home.

CHAPTER FOUR

Choosing a Place to Live

People usually are the happiest at home.

—WILLIAM SHAKESPEARE

After a divorce, many people jump into deciding where to live too quickly, especially when they want to buy a home. Here's my recommendation: for the first year, postpone the big purchase and consider renting. Remain flexible, because the truth is, your future is uncertain, and your budget is probably lower. Further, during that first year, you might find you want to change your style altogether to reflect the changes in your life, or you might meet a new partner who already owns property. Either way, renting provides the flexibility to grow in new directions.

There are many ways home ownership can change in

divorce proceedings, but the two most common are (1) one partner keeps the home, or (2) neither can afford to keep it. In the second case, the house must be sold, with each party splitting the sale price. Whatever the case, if you end up losing the house, it can be hard on your ego. You worked hard to get that house. Maybe you had finally gotten the exact house you wanted. Now, not only is it lost to you, but you also don't have as much money to spend on your next home.

For many people, the next home they buy feels like a step back because it's not as nice as their "real" home. Wherever you end up immediately after your divorce, now is the time to put aside your ego and remind yourself your new living arrangements are only temporary. Be specific, saying something like, "I'll live here two years. By then, I'll have started making money again, so I'll be able to move back in to my favorite part of town."

SERIAL ENTREPRENEUR TURNED SERIAL HOMEOWNER

If you move too fast on the home-ownership front, you can lose a lot. For example, I had a client, a brilliant entrepreneur who came up with business ideas, started companies, ran them for a year or so, and then sold them for a huge profit. He had a long string of success and had amassed a considerable amount of wealth.

He lost half in his divorce.

With momentum from his successful business, he felt comfortable enough to buy another house right after his divorce. I advised him not to do this, but he insisted. That's how he operated, in business and in his life. In fact, he wanted a bigger house than the one he left behind. Now, the Ferrari he leased at $3,000 a month had an $18,000 monthly mortgage to go with it! Unfortunately, when he failed to turn a profit while selling his latest venture, he didn't have enough money to pay the mortgage and had to sell the home at a loss. He even had to give up the lease to the Ferrari. This, of course, put an additional strain on his bank account, but nothing pained him more than the public embarrassment of losing all his cherished status symbols.

The moral of the story is this: don't go big on your first post-divorce house. Your entire life is in flux. Think practically and economically. By making the smart choice now, you'll have greater flexibility to move up later, and you'll feel like you earned the eventual upgrade.

By then, you'll have time to figure out what you want. Where do you want to live? What part of town do you enjoy the most? Do you want to live in a house, or would you prefer a condo? After my divorce, I wasn't sure where I wanted to move in Los Angeles. I considered the beach, downtown, the Westside, or the funkier Eastside. I decided to rent an apartment in Beverly Hills so that my children could continue to stay in the excellent public schools in that area. Renting gave me some time to think things through. I'd just got done splitting up my assets, transitioning to the single life, and sorting out custody with my children. There was no way I had enough time and energy to figure out the best answer to the question of my living situation. As it turned out, my ex-wife later purchased a home in Beverly Hills, and I purchased a home in West Hollywood (the next town over), where my new wife had a business. It all worked out.

PUT A HOLD ON COMMITMENT

I took the rental mentality even further. I rented furniture as well as a home. I knew I wouldn't be on my own forever, so I didn't want to invest in furniture. (After divorce, some people don't even want to think about finding a new partner. I was the opposite. I knew I was better with a partner than I was by myself and was resolved to meet someone new. Just not right away, as we'll discuss in Chapter Seven.) I figured that whoever I met would have her own tastes, possibly even her own house and furniture. She likely wouldn't want any of the furniture I would bring into the marriage.

This knowledge drove two decisions. First, I chose to let my ex-wife keep all the furniture and decorations. I wasn't interested in fighting over couches, dining room tables, and china. None of it was worth what we paid for it, and it probably wouldn't match my new home anyway. Following that thinking, I chose to rent all my furniture, knowing I might not be living in the same place in a year and wanting to maintain flexibility to make appropriate decisions then.

WHAT TO LOOK FOR IN A RENTAL PROPERTY

The first thing to look for in a rental property is the number of bedrooms. If you're the only person living there and you don't have children, all you need is a one-bedroom apartment. Forget the guest room for now; it's just going to stay empty most of the year anyway. Visitors can stay in a hotel or an Airbnb.

IF YOU HAVE CHILDREN

Children require a special set of considerations. For instance, if you have two or more children and they always shared a room at the old place, then it's okay to have them share a room at your new place. In that case, get a two-bedroom apartment. If they've always had their own bedroom, however, then you probably need three bedrooms to maintain some consistency for them.

LOCATION MATTERS

The location of your next home has a huge bearing on your ability to move into the next chapter of your life. Decide where you see yourself fitting in. If you live in a town clogged with traffic and don't want to spend a lot of time commuting, then living near work will be important. If you have children, you'll want them, initially at least, to be somewhere as close to the old neighborhood as possible so it's not a big hassle to get them to school, activities, and sports. Staying close to their friends is also a big must-have for most children.

OTHER CONSIDERATIONS

If you work from home, you need office space. A master bedroom might accommodate that, but if not, find an apartment with another space that allows for productive work time.

Finally, don't forget to consider lifestyle. Do you want to live near the beach, where you won't have a backyard, but you can smell the ocean? Or do you want to live downtown in a high-rise with lots of people and close to any kind of food you want within two blocks? With children, it's important to be near a playground or parks or other outdoor activity destinations.

If you can't find the ideal living situation, remember this

is a short-term solution. In a year or two, you'll be on to better things. In the meantime, find something that's in your budget so you don't stretch yourself too thin when you're trying to rebuild.

HOW TO MAKE YOUR NEW PLACE FEEL LIKE HOME

It takes time for a new living space to feel homey, but you should find yourself settled in within a month or two. To speed this process along with your children, get them involved.

When I first moved from our former house to an apartment, I worried my children wouldn't accept the change, so I decided to make the process more palatable. As we were moving in, I said, "You know, you've got a brand-new, bare room. Let's go out and get new sheets, comforters, and pillows. You can choose everything, including whatever artwork you want to decorate your room." They got so excited about this idea, and it helped the moving-in process run much more smoothly.

So far, so good. However, I was also worried about how they were going to respond to not having their own backyard. All they would get was a shared pool for the whole apartment complex. I never heard them complain once about anything even related to the matter. I don't think it ever bothered them.

Many people want to keep the house or keep their style of living "for the children," but it's always a cop-out. Children are so much more flexible and adaptable than adults. It absolutely does not matter to children where you live. The only thing that matters is that their parent is there, taking care of them, and loving them.

ADJUSTING TO MOVING LONG DISTANCES

If you have children, you have to understand that relocation with your children away from the city, or even a section of the city where they've grown up in, will be difficult. Most courts won't allow you to move away unless you meet specific criteria:

- You cannot get a job anywhere locally, but you do have an opportunity somewhere else.
- No friends or family reside in your current location.
- You can prove you're not trying to move the children away from your ex-spouse.
- You must demonstrate an understanding that this move will come at a great personal sacrifice to you.

As an example of circumstances where a parent was allowed to move with the children, I had a client who was an associate professor of linguistics at the local university. She did not receive tenure there, so she applied elsewhere. Out of the three schools that had an opening for a tenured track position, one was in Florida. It happened she had family in Florida, and this helped persuade the court to approve her request to move.

For the parent who remains in the original location, the typical custody schedule is they get the children for all of the summer, school breaks, and every major holiday weekend, which adds up to roughly 50 percent of the time. It's not as good as seeing your children weekly, but it's the best that a court can do if you or your ex has to make the hard decision of moving out of state.

Just remember, moving is hard even in the best circumstances, so it's important to weigh out your positives and negatives. If you use the kind of chart I recommended in Chapter One, the best move should quickly make itself apparent.

My one experience with a big move came when I was still married and my daughters were one and three. At the time, we were living in suburban southern New Jersey, and I'd made partner at a big law firm in Philadelphia. Many might have said I had it made, but we weren't especially fond of where we lived and were ready for a change. After visiting family in Los Angeles, we weighed out the positives and negatives and decided to make the big move out west. I never once regretted the decision. In the next chapter, we'll discuss how to set up family life in your new home, or your new single life.

CHAPTER FIVE

Building Your New Family Life

Don't worry that your children never listen to you; worry that they are always watching you.

—ROBERT FULGHUM

After divorce, each party has the opportunity to redefine who they are as a parent. Some parents were hardly home before the divorce, while others parented full time. Both can start anew in their parental roles and determine their house rules and expectations, while clearly communicating this to the children involved. Readers without children can skip to Chapter Six.

Getting used to single life after marriage is not easy. In fact, it's stressful, mentally draining, and generally not all that enjoyable. Approaching single parenthood takes that to a whole new level. For better or worse, you don't have to consult with someone else in terms of day-to-day parenting when your children are with you. Maybe you didn't get along with your ex on parenting tactics, and now you don't have that tension, which can be nice. However, at least you had someone to share your ideas with, even if you disagreed. Now that that element is gone, you start to discover that being a single parent is lonely.

The good news is it doesn't have to be. Bring your family members into the child-rearing process. Ask their advice, suggestions, or thoughts on particular issues. If you have a sibling with children, they're a great place to start. If you don't have siblings, consider reaching out to your children's friends' parents.

Whoever you go to, the closer in age that person's own children are to yours, the better. Your parents can also be good for advice, but just know that the generation gap may prove too great an obstacle for certain issues. Even if you have a ten-year-old and your friend has a college-aged child, that friend's advice might already be dated. Parenting standards often change quite a bit over even a decade, so if you can, find someone who is going through a similar experience with children of a similar age.

Another big help is to get input from your own children, especially if they're old enough to have opinions about things. Ask them what they want to do about a given issue, but be clear that you are not abdicating control or giving the child decision-making power. You're asking for their input. "Let's think about what we want to do this weekend, come up with a bunch of ideas, and decide. Is there anything you want to do?" It doesn't have to be a specific activity, but at least try to feel out their goals for how they would like to spend their time with you.

EVALUATE YOUR PARENTING STYLE

If your children feel free enough to give you feedback, that's a great way to learn how they like things done or what makes them the most comfortable. For example, I had a client who couldn't help but hover over his children while they did their homework. Every day when he got home from work, he would sit down at the table with his two children and work through their homework with them. If they'd already done it, he would review it, get out the eraser, and redo things, which his children didn't appreciate.

When he and his wife divorced, he asked his children, "What kinds of things might you want to do differently? I'm not promising we are changing anything, but let's just figure out what is on the list."

To his surprise, they said, "You're driving us crazy with

our homework. We get good grades. We always do our homework and turn it in, but you're treating it like it's this big issue."

He and his children worked out a deal where he would make himself available for homework help from 6:00 and 7:30 each night. If his children had any questions about their homework, they had to come to him then; otherwise, he wasn't going to ask about their homework. If they didn't come to him, he would assume it was done and ready to hand in the next day, and he wasn't going to check on it.

The children didn't have him hovering over them anymore, but they knew they could go to him for homework in a productive, structured way—and often they did just that. This small adjustment took away a tension-filled situation where the dad was always hovering and squashing the children when it came to homework.

As they adopted the new system, even the dad realized he was happier. In fact, he was relieved not to have to hover over his children anymore, because he didn't enjoy it either. Now that he didn't have to come home and immediately sit down and go over homework, he was able to free up all sorts of time for other activities with his children. Even better, he was able to feel proud of his children for the work they were doing on their own.

WHAT TYPE OF PARENT ARE YOU?

When parenting, your goal is to raise independent young adults, not to raise children. It's important to instill in them the confidence and skills to take care of themselves. To do that, most parents adopt one of two broad approaches: authoritative or authoritarian.

So there's no confusion, let me offer a brief explanation of each term. Authoritarian parents believe that children are, by nature, strong-willed and self-indulgent. These parents value obedience to higher authority as a virtue unto itself. Authoritarian parents see their primary job to be bending the will of the child to that of authority—the parent, the church, the teacher, and so on.

Authoritative parents, on the other hand, are also strict, consistent, and loving, but their values and beliefs about parenting and children are markedly different. Authoritative parents are issue-oriented and pragmatic rather than motivated by an external, absolute standard. They tend to adjust their expectations to the needs of the child. They listen to children's arguments, although they may not change their minds. They persuade and explain, as well as punish. In general, they try to balance the responsibility of the child to conform to the needs and demands of others, with the rights of the child to be respected and have their own needs met.

If you're not sure which camp you fall into, online quizzes are a good place to start. It doesn't matter which one you choose. Each will do about the same thing, offering input on what you're doing well, what tactics you should be more aware of, and what approaches you might want to consider changing.

Most experts agree that an authoritative parenting style is more effective than an authoritarian one. In this approach, you still have the final say, but you're open to incorporating your children's ideas into a group problem-solving process, and you won't make rules blindly without reason. Decisions are made with a good explanation as to why you're making them.

The authoritarian, or dictator, approach may accomplish a lot of your parenting goals, but it leaves your children with no say in anything. As a result, they lose out on the opportunity to develop the problem-solving skills they will need as an adult. Everyone needs to know how to sit down with a group, brainstorm solutions, decide on the best one, and agree on their course of action. If your child can learn that at home, they will learn how to incorporate that skill into their own lives as they grow.

REINVENTING WHO YOU ARE AS A PARENT

As we've discussed throughout this book, divorce offers

nearly endless opportunities for personal growth. Here is a second chance to choose what kind of parent you want to be. In my practice, I've noticed that while both spouses often have jobs outside the home, the women still tend to take on much more of the parenting role. As a result, the majority of my male clients have never even experienced what it's like to be a *half-time* parent, much less a full-time one.

After divorce, however, these same men suddenly find that they're responsible for their children a full 50 percent of the time and realize they have to start parenting. It's a wonderful opportunity to rebound, commit to the role, and do it well. Here's my advice to all the ex-spouses— often men—who spent their marriage working too much and not spending enough time at home: take advantage of this new opportunity to spend time with your children.

The best way to do this is to change your work schedule. Plan to work late on days you don't have the children so you can get home early on days you *do* have them. In fact, plan on being home right after school, when children are likely at their most talkative and want to tell you about their day. When they have friends over, pay attention to how they interact with others and make yourself available if they ask you to participate in whatever they're doing.

Naturally, getting more involved with your children's lives

depends greatly on your job flexibility. Some jobs allow for flexible hours, or even part- or full-time telecommuting, but this might not be true for you. If that's the case, see if you can arrange for custody during times of the week where you're more available.

Whatever you do, make sure you're making the most out of this opportunity to impact your children's lives. Remember, spending time with your children is priceless, especially when they're younger. You'll be surprised at how quickly they become independent leaders of their own lives, teenagers who come home from school, retreat to their rooms, and maintain their own social circles. Don't waste the time you have.

SEEK WAYS TO IMPROVE

As a parent, you should always be asking yourself, "Am I doing the best I can? What could I do differently?" Ask yourself that question over and over. For instance, I didn't think making school lunches was a big deal, but after my divorce, I learned there was a lot more to it. Not knowing any better, I simply made my daughters the same kind of standard lunches I grew up on—a sandwich, some fruit, some chips, etc. However, when I started emptying their bags when they came home, most of the food I'd packed was still there.

Shocked and, if I'm being honest, a little hurt, I asked them why they weren't eating their lunches. They were honest with me: they didn't especially like the lunches I packed, so they used parts of their allowance to buy their school lunches instead. Putting pride aside, I realized that if they liked the school lunches better, then I should support that. So we made the change, and just like that, I was out of the school lunch business.

If you're unsure of what to do in situations like this or how you should go about monitoring your own performance, here again, therapists are an invaluable resource. As long as you're willing to be specific about your concerns, a therapist can offer feedback, help in a problem-solving capacity, and work with you to develop alternative approaches.

WHAT CAN I DO ON MY OWN TO BE A BETTER PARENT?

One of the best ways to improve your parenting skills is to ask yourself a lot of questions: What do my children like? What are they good at? What could they use help with? What makes me proud of my children? What makes me frustrated with them?

Look at all the good things and take pride in them, and then quickly move on to any lingering problems or areas they need help with. Take some time with this. Look inside each issue and carefully consider what actions you could take (or encourage your children to take) that will inspire pride rather than frustration.

For example, I had a client who considered herself something of a gourmet. She took pride in the time she spent cooking for her family. She tried to encourage her two young children to taste different foods and learn to differentiate between flavors. Her son was into it and developed a keen sense of taste and smell. Her daughter tried to play along too, but despite her mother's persistence, she just didn't enjoy this as an activity. Eventually, the daughter nearly stopped eating, severely restricting the range of food she would eat. The young girl just didn't feel she could keep up and effectively dropped out of the game.

As we talked about the situation and the effect pressure has on children, I remembered something I learned in college in my developmental psychology course. It turns out, before children will try a new food, most have to see it on their plate six to twelve times first. They have to see it there without being asked to try it so they can feel empowered to make the decision on their own. I used this knowledge when raising my daughters, and now again with my young son. We would put out a plate of, say, chicken, pasta, and broccoli. The first six or seven times, the children wouldn't touch the broccoli, but we wouldn't scold or lecture them about their choice. We wouldn't even point it out. We just left it there. The eighth or ninth time, they started eating the broccoli on their own. If it's food and it's in front of them, they will eventually choose to try it. I can assure you that my young son eats everything on his plate.

After I shared that story with my client, she stopped trying to force her own food interest on her daughter, and the girl eventually started eating again. Once the parent stopped talking about the food all the time, the issue went away.

The end goal is to find a way to change behavior that doesn't intimidate them or make them feel uncomfortable. Let them figure certain activities out for themselves. Too much feedback often will just drive your child to want to tune you out.

HOW TO ESTABLISH HOUSEHOLD RULES AND EXPECTATIONS

The first step in establishing household rules is to take time to yourself and decide what kind of household you want to have. That goes for all the children's behaviors. After they play with toys, are they encouraged to put those toys away, or are they allowed to leave them out until you do a big cleanup at the end of the week? Whatever fits your style, you have to figure out rules like this—such as proper cleanup, eating outside the kitchen, and most importantly, being respectful to each other.

Here are some other kinds of questions you could be asking:

- Are you going to allow name-calling between siblings or demand a certain level of decency?
- When you're talking with your children, do you expect them to look at you and listen, or will you tolerate them looking somewhere else?
- Are your children encouraged to share their food, their ideas, and their fun?
- Do your children say hello and goodbye to visitors? Do they acknowledge the presence of other adults?
- Are your children allowed to bring their phones to the kitchen table while they're eating?

Once you've looked at everything in your household and

decided on what your rules are going to be, communicate your standards clearly to your children. To encourage them to invest in the process, you might even consider involving them in the decision-making process.

If you establish your house rules right up front, you'll find it easier to hold your children to your expectations because they have a stable point of reference. "Kids, remember, we talked about how we wanted this to be a neat household, so if you take something out and use it, put it back when you are done using it instead of leaving it around, so let's do a little cleanup right now." It could be as simple as an after-school routine. When we get home from school, the first thing we do is put our book bags in our rooms and then have a snack. After that, we do our homework, and then we're each permitted a half an hour of iPad time.

Establishing firm ground rules is especially useful for children who feel like everything's up in the air as a result of your divorce. If they come home and have clear expectations, the stage is set for a content and efficient environment, allowing them to settle into their new routines. Most children just want a set of expectations laid out and communicated to them to have stability and certainty. These are the rules we follow, this is the way we're going to live, and if we follow these rules and engage in these behaviors, we'll all be happy at home.

SETTING RULES IMPROVES COMMUNICATION AND DECISION-MAKING

If you don't have a clear set of rules, you set yourself up to have to make new decisions every day about what your children can or can't do. Establishing rules, communicating them, and reinforcing them saves you a lot of the mental labor of being reactionary.

Established rules also help you be consistent. Without a rule, your decision-making process might be relatively consistent, but it's not guaranteed. If your child realizes that eight times out of ten they get one answer, but two times they get a different answer they like better, they will keep testing you on that issue. That's what children do. But if they get the same answer ten out of ten times, they quickly learn there's no winning the argument.

Many people are afraid of making decisions, so they delay making them or try to buy time to think about it some more. That rarely helps. The key to decision-making is thinking in a systematic way. Make a decision without delaying, and then see if that decision worked out. If you make a wrong decision, you will realize it relatively quickly. However, if that happens, you can just make a different decision and see if that works.

Making a wrong choice isn't a crime, and it doesn't mean you failed. It just means you tried something, it didn't work, and now you're going to try something else. Now that you know one particular solution doesn't work, you can cross it off the list and move to your next solution until you get it right.

TAKING OWNERSHIP OF NEW PARENTING AND HOME RESPONSIBILITIES

Most people know what they know and are comfortable with that. However, just realize that your new parenting responsibilities and homelife bring up new challenges. If you don't know how to do something, remember that you have options:

1. 1. Soldier on and figure it out yourself.
2. 2. Ask someone in your support system.
3. 3. Track down answers online.

For instance, let's say cooking isn't your thing. Local bookstores and libraries are packed with cookbooks on preparing meals in less than thirty minutes. That's a great place to start putting together meals for you and your children. Online, you have a near-endless supply of resources for healthy, easy meal prep. YouTube still amazes me with its instant-access answers and video instruction on almost anything. I can find an old Groucho Marx clip one day and learn how to wire a security camera to an old electrical outlet the next. That said, if you're not interested in DIY efforts, plan to leave space in your budget to secure help.

Housekeeping, for example, is something many people hire out. While you as a single parent are ultimately responsible for what goes on in the house, it doesn't mean you have to be the only one who physically does each chore. If you hate grocery shopping, there are services that will do that for you. Not a fan of laundry? Hire a service or bring in a housekeeper. You can even order preportioned meals and recipes from services like Blue Apron that only require cooking. If there's money in the budget, it's well worth it to hire someone else to do everyday tasks so you can focus on parenting.

AN AU PAIR GIVES A PARENT MORE CHILD TIME

I represented a wife and mom who had ascended to an executive-level position in her career. In typical fashion, her schedule was usually overbooked. While she had hired someone to pick up her children from school, she found that when she got home, she still had too many things preventing her from spending constructive time with her children. Helping with a school project, for instance, meant shuttling to the store for supplies and myriad other small tasks before actually being able to start the work.

This frustrated executive eventually looked into hiring an au pair to handle everyday, time-consuming chores. For those unfamiliar with the term, an au pair is typically a foreign student in the year off between high school graduation and beginning college. They come to the United States to live with a family, and while there, provide thirty-five hours per week of childcare.

The mom worked with the au pair by listing specific duties for her au pair to follow, and this person quickly made the executive's life more efficient.

After hearing this, I asked the executive if having an au pair was cheating. After all, wasn't the au pair essentially doing the executive's job as a mother? Wasn't she missing out on parenting? She explained that, yes, she had the au pair do all the busy work, like driving the carpool, toting the children to an activity and back, or pinballing around town collecting school supplies. However, the executive made the point that it actually made her more effective as a mother since it let her enjoy their shared activities and homework time with her children.

MANAGING CUSTODY AND COPARENTING COMPLICATIONS

Whenever children are in the mix, the court will decide on a custody schedule for you and your ex-spouse. You may not like what the court decides, but here's my advice:

for the first six to twelve months, just follow the schedule. Don't try to change timing or switch days. Don't negotiate between Thursdays and Fridays. Don't ask for special favors because you have Dodgers tickets one night. Save the negotiation for later.

Remember, you just negotiated your way out of a marriage, a process that leaves most people unhappy and burned out. Most likely, there is still some bad blood between you and your ex, and it's best to let those feelings die down before you start throwing in spontaneous schedule changes. After six to twelve months, you and your ex will be more relaxed and settled into your new routine.

This approach certainly helped me in the year after my divorce. Sure, I might have been a divorce lawyer and former therapist who knew what to expect, but I still couldn't stop my emotions from getting the best of me. For months, I was deeply wrapped up in custody considerations. I didn't want to give away any of my time because I didn't want my children to think I didn't care. Despite how strongly I felt, I made sure to stick with the schedule until I calmed down.

Once you and your ex are used to the schedule, shared custody becomes more like a business relationship. Approaching interactions in this way keeps things on an even keel and avoids the tendency for emotions to fuel any fires.

For better or for worse, your ex will likely remain the same person after the divorce. They won't suddenly become more likable. But if you can keep a little emotional distance, it's no big deal to switch weekends with the children.

I had a client whose ex-wife had a flair for the dramatic. She turned every small disagreement into a big deal. For the first six months after their divorce, he forwarded me every email he got from her so I could help him figure out the reason for the mail. Somewhere in all the ranting was a reason, and when I found it, I would provide my client with a one-sentence reply. Eventually, he learned how to process these messages himself, and as he stopped being defensive, she stopped attacking.

He and his ex never would have reached that point if he hadn't treated her messages like a business task. If you find yourself in a similar situation with your ex, ask yourself, "What do I have to decide here, and how do I do it in the simplest, most professional manner?" With practice, it shouldn't take long for you to identify and politely respond to the core issue.

ENCOURAGE CHILDREN TO WORK WITH EACH PARENT DIRECTLY

"I came home and mom yelled at me, and I don't think she should do that. Can you talk to her?"

"Dad still works late and he's not there when I get to his house."

Your children will most likely have trouble at times with their interactions with your ex. Your first impulse will probably be to get involved. Don't.

As a single parent, you have to stay away from those issues. Encourage your children to express themselves to the other parent and try to work things out on their own. You can offer advice in this regard, but don't make any attempt to try and change your ex-spouse's behavior. Nothing good will ever come from that.

Besides, the more you encourage your children to solve their problems for themselves, the better they'll get at it. Every adult needs to understand how to deal with a potentially difficult adult—people who disagree, who make snap decisions, who won't listen to reason, or who act against their own self-interest—so they might as well start practicing now. If children learn at a young age how to deal effectively with their parents, it prepares them well for their future.

Respect your ex's custody time with the children. Don't focus on what your children do and who they do it with when they're not with you. You might think some things aren't perfect, but as long as your children are not in danger, you have no business interfering.

If your ex has 50 percent of the time, they're in charge during that time. Period. Don't ask the children what they did at mom's house or where dad took them for dinner. If you can't control it, there's no reason to worry about it. All those questions will do is lead to consternation in the family.

After I separated from my first wife, for instance, she eventually found a new partner. For the children's first Hanukkah with him, he planned a scavenger hunt. This ran counter to what I would have preferred. I don't treat Hanukkah as a big holiday, and at first, I was upset that he was planning activities like this for my children. For a moment, I even thought I should do something about it, but fortunately, logic prevailed. I talked to my father about the situation, and he reminded me of his favorite quote from the movie *The Godfather*: "It's not personal, Sonny. It's strictly business." My father has reminded me of this saying many, many times over the years, and he has always been right. And what he meant was that I needed to step back and treat the incident as a business transaction. If my children enjoyed the time they were spending with my ex's new partner, that was all that mattered. I wasn't being replaced as a parent, and I certainly wasn't the only one allowed to have fun with my children. None of those ego statements would have helped me as a parent, and they certainly wouldn't have helped with my children.

WHAT'S THE RIGHT AMOUNT OF INVOLVEMENT WITH MY EX?

In most cases, the vibe between ex-spouses isn't the best. If live conversations lead to bickering, it's perfectly fine to avoid them. Use text and email instead, and navigate your custody schedule wisely. Most parent-to-parent child transfers happen through school: one parent drops them off in the morning, and the other picks up in the afternoon. That way, neither you nor your children need to be exposed to the tension between you and your ex-spouse. Plus, it gives your children an entire school day to reset. If there's no way for the parents to coordinate in such a manner, consider using a babysitter or nanny as an intermediary in order to avoid any potential problems.

PLAN FOR YOUR CHILDLESS DAYS

On the days you don't have your children, it's up to you how to fill that time. Maybe those are the days you work later or explore new activities you always wanted to try, but didn't have the time or courage. This is your time to find a new social outlet or a sport—or maybe even write that novel.

I know of a few people who used the time to learn new skills and share their recently acquired talents with their children. One person, for instance, would take cooking classes on Monday and then make their children fun new meals later in the week. Often, they would even get their children involved in the cooking process.

While learning new skills is almost always worth it, it's best to delay sharing or showing them off to your children until you've had a chance to practice and become proficient, because that can backfire. During one case I worked on, a particularly aggressive custody battle, I saw it happen. As a routine part of the proceedings, a psychologist was sent to the father's home to assess the environment. The father wanted so badly to impress the psychologist that he thought it would be a good idea to bake some brownies with his children. The problem was, he'd never baked brownies before and had no idea how to make that happen. The mixer broke, brownie mix flew all over the kitchen, and the pan he bought didn't fit in the oven. He and his children had plenty of fun laughing about the incident later, but at the time, it was a tense, stressful mess.

Along with reinventing who you are as a parent, divorce also offers the opportunity to redefine your social life and circle of friends. Your relationships will change. Most likely, your friend list needs revisiting. You might be friends with a couple you used to hang out with as a couple with your ex. As a single person, are you still friends with both of them? Either of them? Now is the time to decide who you want to spend your time with. Maybe you have ten close friends but only get together with two of them. In the next chapter, we'll explore ways to take the opportunity for reflection that life has given you and decide which friends bring you the most enjoyment or positivity.

CHAPTER SIX

———

Redesigning Your Social Life

Lots of people want to ride with you in the limo, but what you want is someone who will take the bus with you when the limo breaks down.

—OPRAH WINFREY

When you were married, you spent your time and energy on your relationship with your spouse. With that person absent from your life, you may have a lot of energy to spare, so you may as well spend it on something productive—like reestablishing your social life. You've figured out where to live and all the logistics surrounding your children. Now, it's time to focus on you. Before seeking out a new romantic partner, take some time to strengthen your friendships. You will find this investment invaluable later on when romance blooms again in your life.

Once again, your first step is to create another list. Write out all of your friends on one side and what you do together on the other. Now, ask yourself *why* you spend this time with each friend. Does this person make your life better? Do you hang out with them for stability and familiarity, or do they truly make you happy? For example, perhaps you have a good friend from college, but you don't have much in common anymore. In fact, whenever you get together, all you do is talk about the old times. This might be okay every now and then, but most likely, you don't want that person in your core circle.

Similarly, friends you used to see with your ex as a couple might now be uncomfortable hanging out with you by yourself. That's okay too. If that person is uncomfortable and you don't have anything to add to that friendship, it's okay to let it go.

Your goal with this exercise is to seek balance where you can. You're not looking to eliminate every imperfect person from your circle of friends, but you are trying to narrow your focus to the people who consistently offer you the most valuable and meaningful experiences. Just because you've been in a friendship with someone for a long time doesn't mean you still need to actively maintain it.

This approach might feel somewhat calculated and

systematic at first, but I know it works, because I did it. The result was a list of people who made me feel better, helped me enjoy myself, or gave me good feedback, and I could do the same things for them. By choosing to spend my time with them, I ensure that I don't spread myself too thin.

EVALUATING YOUR FRIENDS

Think about each person on your list. How do they talk to you and treat you? Do they behave differently when you're alone or with a group of people? Do they enjoy trying new activities with you, or do they only want to hang out on their own terms?

During my own evaluation process, for example, my thoughts kept coming back to an old high school friend. We had kept in touch for years—through college, grad school, and my marriage. Though we talked occasionally, we had grown apart. My friend played guitar in one garage cover band after another and dropped out of college to continue that hobby. The only way I was able to maintain our friendship was through his gigs, but his band usually wouldn't start playing until ten o'clock, the venue was always dark and smoky, and I usually had to go to work the next day.

Eventually, there came a point when the inconvenience

outweighed any enjoyment I was receiving. I asked him if we could start doing different things, but he didn't want to. He had no interest in hiking, sports, or other social activities. I was sad to do it, but it was time to let that friendship go. We may have known each other a long time, but forcing myself to spend time at his gigs took time away from my other interests, and investing that time didn't make sense anymore.

In my case, my friend and I had simply outgrown each other. In other cases, you may discover that some relationships are actually more harmful than good. Whatever the situation, don't settle for less or for what you always had. You'll need space on your list for the new friends you're going to make as part of the moving-on process, so you might as well start making that space now.

HOW DO FRIENDS DROP FRIENDS?

There is an ebb and flow to every friendship, both the good and the bad. A close friend at one point in your life could be little more than an acquaintance later on.

If you don't believe me, here's a little exercise you can try. If you first got married five or more years ago, think back to all the people you invited to your wedding. If you got married again today, how many of those same people would you invite? All of them? Half of them? None of them? Usually when I ask this question, most people say about half. The other half might have meant something once upon a time, but that time has passed.

While many unsatisfying relationships end naturally, some require a more conscious decision. I had a client whose stepmother always dwelled on the negative side of a story, finding the black cloud in everything rather than the silver lining. It took a while for him to realize the impact her pessimism was having on his life, but eventually he got tired of dealing with it. When he asked for my advice, I told him to stop calling, stop returning her calls, and stop setting up plans. He did, and eventually she got the message.

As you begin the process of letting certain friends go, keep in mind that you'll probably find yourself on the receiving end as well. Some friends, for instance, might choose to remain close with your ex instead of you. If that happens, don't take it personally. There are plenty of people out there you can hang out with who would happily choose you over someone else. Anyone not willing to do that is best to let go anyway.

REPAIRING BROKEN FRIENDSHIPS

You may have lost friends who weren't comfortable relating to you in your relationship with your ex-spouse. People don't want to be around a negative relationship. Some of them may have disappeared from your life because they didn't enjoy being around your ex-spouse. Most likely, they didn't like the person you became at that time either.

If you lost people you valued over the course of your former marriage and you would like to reconnect, don't hesitate. Send an email, a text, or a call. Say something to the effect of, "Hey, we haven't talked in a long time. I've been thinking about what's been going on in my life and about my friends, and I think we grew apart because of my former relationship. I'd like to get together some time."

Nine times out of ten, those people are so happy to get that message that they'll rush out to meet you anywhere you'd like. When you get the chance to talk things out, just be honest about what you did and tell them you're sorry about it. Let them know you realize you made some bad decisions in a tough time of your life, but you're past that now. Often, they'll offer some apology of their own and then proceed to tell you how much they missed you and the person you were before things turned bad.

Whatever they tell you, embrace the learning opportunity. We often don't realize how we affect other people when we're caught up in our own lives. Luckily, genuine friends have a way of jumping right back in to being connected.

HOW ELSE CAN I REVAMP MY SOCIAL LIFE?

It might not seem like it, but this is an exciting time for you. What did you always want to do but didn't because you were married? Maybe there were activities your ex-spouse wasn't interested in and you just never pursued them. If you enjoyed sailing, for instance, but your spouse always got seasick, you either had to go without them (which is a fast track to trouble in paradise) or choose to do something else. The latter is usually the right decision in a marriage, but you're not married anymore. Here's your chance to try out new sports, new hobbies, new social activities, and new exercise classes. With all those options, you're bound to meet plenty of new and interesting people in the process.

If you're especially interested in making new connections during this time, consider more formalized options, such as meet-up groups. For instance, I have a client who joined a newly single men's golfing group. They would all meet on a weekday, split up into fours, and hit the ball around. Despite his reservations about joining a "divorced dads" group, once he got there, he realized how valuable it was to spend time with people going through the same process as him. He also enjoyed that the group wasn't focused on discussing the members' failed relationships. They were there to golf, and they just happened to be newly divorced.

My client found it reaffirming to know that what he was

dealing with was real and not all in his head. Everyone was in a similar situation and was experiencing a similar set of emotional responses. Sure, some people dealt with those emotions in ways that he might not have agreed with, but even then, he said talking with them made for a good learning experience.

As another option that fulfills a similar social need, I've had clients who made friends with the newly divorced parents of their children's friends. In many ways, these parents make ideal friends. Because they have children the same age as yours, they are probably dealing with the same social and schooling issues that you are. Additionally, they are probably doing these things alone, as you might be. What better type of person to learn from? If you happen to have any other shared interests, that makes it all the better. In general, my clients who have taken this route have found it an easy way to connect with others and bond over shared experiences.

I'M AN INTROVERT—MAKING
NEW FRIENDS ISN'T EASY

Many people are introverts. For them, it simply isn't easy getting out there to meet new friends. I'm a natural introvert myself and prefer to stay home when I can. After my divorce, I knew I would have to work harder at making new connections. In such circumstances, I've found that making and holding myself to a calendar helps get me out of the house.

Most of us have some type of calendar on our phone or computer. As a lawyer, mine is constantly alerting me that I have fifteen minutes until my next phone call or thirty minutes to my next meeting. I also use my calendar to remind myself to write my blogs and articles on time, so I dedicate an hour on the first Monday of each month to writing. The set time helps me stay on track and promote my work.

You can do the same thing with your social life. Schedule outings and events that get you out there. Put that new exercise class on your calendar and stick to it. Many nights, you might not want to go out, but putting important activities on a calendar gives you extra motivation to follow through with them.

Using the calendar to set social goals will likely feel awkward and forced at first. You might object that meeting new friends should be a natural process. There's still room in your life for natural friendships to occur, but if you have a tool to help nudge you in the right direction, why waste it? Besides, after a while, things won't feel so programmatic, but rather a natural part of your routine.

Another strategy that I used was to give structure to the experience. I wouldn't worry about meeting every single person during an event or activity. Instead, I simply planned to meet and talk to one person. I would introduce myself and learn a little about them. Then, if I enjoyed talking with them, I would know I had something to look forward to next time. If I didn't enjoy talking to them, I would move on to another person. Either way, once I had talked to and really taken the time to meet just one person, I gave myself permission to leave. Oftentimes, however, the experience was so rewarding that I stayed and met additional people.

THINGS TO BE AWARE OF WHEN MAKING NEW FRIENDS

The first thing to remember when meeting new people is *not* to ramble on about your divorce or how you feel about your ex: (1) that person might know your ex, and (2) digging up the past is no way to move forward. It doesn't help to be looking over your shoulder at your past, talking about what went wrong or what you should have done differently. New friendships don't typically start off well if they're based on complaining or negativity.

Remember that many new people you meet might also be in a transitional stage. Some friendships will be short lived while others could become more enduring. Whatever the case, some people come in and out of our lives. They could be helpful and fun to be with for a while, but when situations change, it's okay to move on. In fact, it's part of the natural progression.

I had a couple of close friends, for example, who I spent a lot of time with after my divorce. We were all close for a year or two as they helped me learn the dating scene, but eventually, I got into a relationship, and afterward, we didn't have as much in common. Everyone moved on, and there were no hard feelings.

In the next chapter, we'll talk about moving on to find new romantic interests. Hopefully by now, you're settled in to a comfortable place in life and ready to use everything you learned in earlier chapters of this book to find what makes you happy.

CHAPTER SEVEN

Reentering the Dating Scene

What is a date, really, but a job interview that lasts all night? The only difference is there aren't many job interviews where there's a chance you'll end up naked.

—JERRY SEINFELD

One of the most crucial elements of moving on is finding a new relationship that doesn't repeat the mistakes of the previous one. As a general rule, I recommend taking a year before reentering the dating scene. In the meantime, make a list of all the things you want in a new partner, from appearances and character traits to habits and hobbies. Further, it's important to reflect on what you contributed to your previous relationship rather than blaming everything that went wrong on your ex.

Getting back in the dating scene causes the most anxiety after marriage. If you've been married for some time, the dating scene has likely changed since you were last out there. When I met my second wife, dating apps and sites like eHarmony were just starting to emerge. From the fifties to the late nineties, the general process of meeting and dating people followed relatively the same formula: you met people through your friends, school, work, church, and the like, and when you did meet someone, it was an exclusive deal. You'd date someone for a while, and then if it didn't work out, you'd break up and find someone else.

It was a bit of a shock when I reentered the dating scene after my divorce. Modern-day dating had changed considerably, and that was a decade ago. It's even more different now thanks to the presence of social media, online dating, and other web-based relationship options. Today, it's not uncommon for people to juggle more than one partner or relationship at once to determine which is the best fit. For people like me, modern dating sometimes feels complicated, expensive, and exhausting. Who has the time or presence of mind to try and keep multiple relationships going at once?

If you've been out of the dating scene awhile like I was, you might find yourself having a similar reaction, which is all the more reason to take things slowly at first. Take the time to learn the new protocols. You'll likely find that even basic dating activities are different than you were used to. Drinks, dinner, and a movie may feel like the default, but depending on where you live—West Coast, East Coast, big city, or rural area—it might not be anymore. As you research the latest courtship rituals, remember that you don't have to try them all. Look at your options and decide on the approaches you're most comfortable with.

When I was new on the dating scene, I learned that dinner and a movie don't happen until a little later on. Today's early dates are often centered around a daytime activity, such as meeting for coffee or a quick lunch, going on a hike, or enjoying other outdoor activities. Knowing this might not seem like a big deal, but by ignoring standard practices, you risk putting out the wrong signals. For instance, asking someone to a concert on a first or second date could be off-putting.

I learned the value of knowing the rules early on in my courtship with my wife. After our second or third date, she asked what I wanted to do the next time we got together. I suggested ordering in Chinese food and watching a movie.

Her reply was, "You understand that ordering in and watching a movie when you're dating is totally different than when you're married, right?"

I looked at her bewildered.

Patiently, she explained that, for a dating couple, that kind of evening plan typically holds an expectation of sex. Being relatively new to the situation, I was clueless and fortunate she saved me from a potentially embarrassing night.

COMBATTING FEARS

My suggestion to stay home and watch a movie was a simple miscue, but it's the kind of mistake many of us are terrified to make in new relationships. You're afraid to admit you don't know how to do something because that might make you look foolish. You're afraid of saying something that doesn't make sense because you might seem too old-fashioned or out of touch with reality. Other fears creep in there too: fear of rejection, fear of wasting your time with someone who's not a good match, fear of saying the wrong thing, etc.

We're all afraid we're going to say or do something that will make us unappealing to our potential partner, but we shouldn't be. The truth is, you're probably going to be rejected—more than once, in fact, so prepare yourself for it. You're highly unlikely to meet the right person on the first try, and that's a good thing. Finding the right partner, someone who is a good match for you in a variety of ways, *should* take several tries before you get it right. As much as you can, practice putting aside your ego and accept that fairy tale romances are not an everyday thing.

To ease your transition through the awkward stages of dating, it's important to reach out to friends for context. Find people who are currently out there dating, or were recently dating, and learn from them. They can give you tips on the latest dating trends, acceptable behaviors, even expectations on paying for dinner. More traditional women, for example, may still expect to be treated to nights out and have the door opened for them, but many others prefer outings where the financial burden is shared equally. Start with what you're comfortable with and build on that.

I approached this challenge by finding what I called my "Three Wise Men." One was a divorced friend who had been dating three or four years looking for the right person. Another was single and had never been married. The third had been divorced years before and vowed he would never remarry and was content being a serial dater. Each offered a different perspective that I valued. After talking with them, I would weigh out their suggestions and opinions, and then move forward with a strategy I was comfortable with. Sometimes, the path I took more or less followed one of my Three Wise Men's advice. Other times, I took a path all my own.

PREPARING TO DATE AGAIN

Whether your divorce was relatively easy or a knock-down, drag-out fight, ending a marriage comes with considerable emotional tension. You need time to process, which is why I recommend taking a year or so away from dating to concentrate on building your new life.

Your first goal during this time is to shed the emotional baggage that came with your prior relationship and the corresponding divorce. Once again, talking with a therapist can be invaluable in this process. At first, you'll find it easy to focus these sessions all on your ex. It's *always* easier to talk about the things you don't like about other people than it is to talk about yourself. However, eventually you'll want to transition from airing out your grievances with your ex to taking a good, long look at yourself. What do you want to change about yourself so you don't repeat the same mistakes in your next relationship? How can you become a better partner? Until you realize your role in the end of your former marriage, you risk moving from one bad relationship to the next.

During this period, also remember that feeling bad about your marriage usually goes along with feeling bad about yourself. That's why I've encouraged you through the previous chapters to take the opportunity to revamp your style, consider where you live, think about how you run your household, and take stock of your friendships. With each of these elements, ask yourself what these choices say about you. Are they an accurate reflection of who you are *right now*, or are they merely a reflection of who you were in the past? For instance, when was the last time you switched up your hairstyle or changed your wardrobe? When I asked my own friends about my style choices, for instance, they didn't hesitate to suggest I ditch the "dad jeans" and Birkenstocks that I'd worn almost like a uniform for ten years. It was time to update my look.

Investigate the kinds of social groups you think will be most conducive to dating once you're ready. Spend time both with friends who are in relationships and friends who are not, and learn from all of them. Get your feet wet trying new things without the pressure of making a one-on-one connection. Don't worry about meeting that special someone every time you go out. If you're creating regular opportunities for yourself, you'll connect with someone else eventually.

WHAT SHOULD I LOOK FOR IN A NEW PARTNER?

Before you start testing the dating waters, it's a good idea to have an idea of the kind of partner you're looking for. Make a list of the ten most important characteristics you want in a new partner. If you find yourself listing out more than that, see if you can narrow it down. After all, you don't want someone exactly like you, and you don't want to be held accountable to finding someone who meets a long list of trivial requirements. You may want to find someone who offers something new that complements your inherent attributes.

In fact, remembering to be flexible and open to new experiences is a big part of this exercise. Here's a chance to meet a new kind of person. To do this, think back to when you met your first spouse. Did you have a specific type of person in mind back then? If so, what were those expectations, and how much do they matter to you now? One or two elements might be the same, but most likely you'll be looking at an entirely new list.

As you explore different attributes, consider the following broad categories:

- Physical appearance
- Hobbies and favorite activities
- Who is in their circle of friends
- Their relationship to their family of origin
- How they treat other people, both "equals" and people who work for them
- Their feelings about religion
- How they handle money

Your goal is to strike a balance between being too critical and not critical enough, all while keeping an eye on any big red flags. If you don't like your partner's friends, for example, or you have wildly different approaches to handling money, then it might be difficult building a relationship long term. While it's important to be aware of potential incompatibilities like this, be careful not to be hypercritical either. If you hold out for everything on your list and write off anyone who misses the mark, you'll never meet the right person. No one is perfect (including you).

As you learn to strike that balance, think of your list like a test in grade school. If someone misses one out of ten, they're still at 90 percent, which is good enough for an A-minus. Even a seven or eight out of ten is a solid score, enough to put your potential partner way ahead of the game. Remember as well that your list will likely evolve as you actually begin dating, so don't get too attached to it.

THE CHILD FACTOR

Does your potential partner already have children, want to have children, or want to have more children? Do they want to get to know your children? Some people don't want to be a stepparent to someone else's children while others are happy to. Some don't want to start new families, while others are eager to. Whatever the case, questions surrounding children have the potential to be a huge source of tension in a relationship, especially if they're not addressed early. It's critical to figure out where both of you stand on the child issue, which means being up front with each other early on.

In my own experience, I was lucky to have a partner so up front about her own desires in this department. On our very first date, my now-wife asked me if I wanted to have more children. I replied that I was excited to have more, which was a good thing, too, since she told me it was important to her in a relationship. There was one perfect match on our list.

CONSIDER OTHER LIFE COMPONENTS

Other variables to consider include family dynamics and careers. Is the person you're dating close with their family, do they keep in touch, or do they not interact at all? None of these options is better than another, and the answer to this question might not matter to you either. Here, the question you have to ask yourself is whether that person's approach to family matches your desired way of life.

Career considerations are important to some and not at all to others. Often, people don't care what their partner does for a living but hope that they enjoy doing it. However, if you find your partner's work despicable, the relationship probably won't work.

For example, as I got to know my future wife, I learned that her family runs a restaurant and that she runs the catering and special events department. She's always making menus, planning parties, ordering balloon arrangements, and trying out new cookie recipes. It's all wonderful, happy-occasion stuff.

I, on the other hand, practice divorce. My day is often filled with negativity. There's no winning; there's just getting through it.

In that regard, some might say we come from two different worlds. In a way, I'll admit that we do, but we each understand what the other person does. She never thought she'd date a divorce lawyer, and I never thought I'd marry a party planner, but we are grateful to have found each other just the same.

HOW TO START LOOKING FOR SOMEONE NEW

If you're willing to take advantage of today's online dating sites and social media lifestyle, it's an easy way to get back into the dating game. Match, JDate, and other online sites have improved immensely over the past decade in their ability to match potential partners.

Make use of these digital options, but don't make this your primary strategy. Consider your real-life social networks as well. Share the list of what you're look-ing for in a partner with other people in your life such as friends, family members, and trusted coworkers. Relying on people you trust is typically a comfortable route to take. For me, I found the experience to be a warmer, more positive way to meet people than get-ting an email or text. If nothing else, your common acquaintance provides you with a great conversation starter.

WAITING NO LONGER

I met Carol through a third party, in a most unexpected way. It started when I began attending gatherings with one of my Three Wise Men. He was part of a group of guys who met once a month on a new moon, built a fire on the beach, hung out, and talked about whatever was going on in their lives. They formed their own little support group from many walks of life—old and young, married and unmarried, lawyers, doctors, carpenters, and plumbers. Each time I joined them, I gleaned more insight into what I wanted in a partner.

At some point, one of them said, "You have to put what you're looking for out into the universe, and it will open you up to meeting the right person." It sounded like a whole lot of nonsense to me at the time, but I tried it anyway. I half expected a sign from the heavens or angel music announcing an amazing new person in my life, but it didn't quite follow that script.

Instead, I met my wife in a therapist's waiting room.

We didn't know it, but at the time, Carol and I both happened to be seeing the same therapist. I was trying to figure out what I was looking for in a partner and how to find it while she was trying to figure out what she could be doing differently after a string of unsuccessful relationships.

The day we met was a fluke. Normally, I had a standing appointment early on Tuesday mornings. That week, however, I had to reschedule for Wednesday. I arrived to my appointment at what I thought was the agreed-upon time, but when I entered the office, I found Carol sitting patiently in the waiting room.

This was odd right off the bat. Psychologists stagger their patients to ensure privacy. You're never supposed to run into anyone else. Even when I practiced as a psychologist, I never had two people waiting at the same time. Yet there I was, sitting with a complete stranger, waiting for the same therapist.

We each had gotten there early (another item on my list was punctuality), and we began talking almost immediately. Carol was friendly, outgoing, upbeat, and just plain charming. In just a few minutes, I was completely interested in this new person, and I wanted to learn more about her. As it turned out, the mishap was my fault. I was an hour early, and when the therapist came to the door, she politely asked me to come back later.

I had been in therapy for about a year, and recently, we had progressed to the point of, "When are you going to start dating? It's about time to get started."

In my session later that day, I admitted that I had been seeing a couple of different people, but I wasn't interested in talking about them. Instead, I told the therapist, "I know you can't tell me anything about that woman in the waiting room today, but that's someone I think I'd want to ask out." Unsurprisingly, my therapist didn't offer much of a reply, and I didn't think about the encounter again.

Two days later, my therapist called and left me a voicemail that said, "About that person you might want to meet...you should probably give her a call. I can't say anything more." And she hung up.

In the psychotherapist-patient confidence and ethical practice world, that's an unusual message to hear, but it worked. I found the mystery woman online through her business, sent her a message, and waited to hear back. After hearing nothing all weekend, I figured she wasn't interested.

As I soon discovered, she was plenty interested. She just didn't check that account very often. When she finally saw my message that Monday, I received a wonderful reply telling me how glad she was that I had contacted her and that she had also felt a spark during our chance encounter.

I was so overwhelmed by her response that I didn't know what to write back. So I didn't. Instead, I left work, drove to her restaurant, and called her from the street. "I'm out front. Why don't you come out?" She was impressed I was the kind of guy who would just jump in his car to come meet someone like her. I'm grateful it made such a good impression, but the truth is, except for that day, I hadn't been that type of person before or since. I'd only done it because I couldn't figure out what else to do! Whatever the case, it worked. From there, I asked her if she wanted to grab a bite to eat, which she did (at her restaurant), and then we made plans to go to dinner a couple of nights later.

Life's turns are fascinating. I never expected to meet someone in a waiting room, and it never would have happened if I hadn't screwed up my appointment time. Sometimes, the stars *do* align, and you just have to be open to it.

STACKING UP AGAINST THE LIST

So how did my future wife compare to my list of ideal partner traits? Not bad at all. Out of ten want-to-haves, she hit eight of them. I was looking for someone friendly and outgoing, who treated everyone with respect. She doesn't look down on people or have any biases. Her family is close, and she works with her mother and a sister as owners of a restaurant. My family all lives on the East Coast, so I wanted someone with a strong, local family.

There were only a couple of things on my list that didn't match. I thought I wanted someone with their own children so we'd be equally experienced in parenthood, but she didn't have children. The other nonmatch was financial. Carol was much more fiscally conservative than I was.

From working with all types of clients, I knew the money issue wouldn't be a deal breaker. Some of my clients and their partners never worry about money. They both make plenty and don't even look at what they spend or what they save until the end of the year. Others make use of a strict budget, setting aside money for savings, entertainment, and emergencies. We actually spent a good deal of time ahead of our marriage talking about how we would handle money—both how we would save and how we would spend. I made myself much more conservative to match her style, and it has worked out to this day.

We also worked through another challenge on our way to marriage: a few of her preconceived ideas on being a parent were what I would call "slightly unrealistic." But that was okay. I knew that most people prior to having children have a set of ideas that change significantly once they have children. So I didn't spend a lot of time correcting her. I let it ride until we had a child of our own and it all fell into place.

The point being, even with things that don't match or you don't agree on, discussing it up front lets you find a way through.

HOW DO I GET BETTER AT DATING?

There's no getting around it: the first couple of relationships you have that don't work out will come with hurt feelings. It's not pleasant, but it's part of learning as you go, being open to meeting others, and adjusting expectations. There are a great many failed relationships in dating's early stages and you simply funnel it down until it clicks and you meet someone you want to be with. To make sure you're moving in the right direction, here are some other things to keep in mind.

REVISE YOUR LIST

You have to be willing to change your list in small ways as you move into a new relationship. If someone doesn't meet a trait on your list but has a different characteristic that you realize is important, simply edit your list. By revisiting and revising your list along the way, you'll improve your judgment process and head off potential failed relationships before they ignite and quickly fizzle.

For example, I had a female client who was a runner. She enjoyed casual running for fitness and spending time outside. She was sure she wanted to meet someone with that same interest and expected it to be great, but it turned out to be the opposite. She found a guy who ran marathons—six marathons a year, in fact. At any given moment, he was either training for a marathon or recovering. When they ran together, she couldn't keep up, and he wasn't willing to slow down. Because he had to stick with a specific mileage and pace, she ended up finishing every run alone. She hated the fact that he always ran ahead and wasn't considerate toward her, so she vowed to stop dating runners.

KEEP A LIGHT HEART

Whatever happens, don't let it bring you down. Remember the odds are that the first date will probably not lead to marriage. In fact, the second, fifth, and fifteenth dates probably won't either. Failed relationships are part of the process of learning who you want to be with (and who you don't), but keep in mind that every relationship offers something, even if it doesn't work out. When a relationship ends, reflect back on the fun you had, the new things you learned, and the new activities you tried. Practicing this kind of reflection keeps you more positive than you would be it if you look at every relationship as just another in a string of failures.

I learned the value of rolling with things way back on that day in the waiting room. Soon after I met Carol, I told her about the Three Wise Men and all their rules for dating. For instance, according to the Wise Men, if I went on a date and had a great time, I was supposed to wait at least a day to call or text so I didn't appear too interested. I told her I didn't want to wait to call her, and she said she didn't want me to either.

"Forget what everyone else says," she said. "I hate the waiting around time for the next call too."

From there, we decided to ditch all the rules and build our relationship on honest communication. If we wanted to go out again, we'd set up the next date at the end of the date we were on. On that particular night, we agreed to meet in two days to play tennis. As a result, I didn't have to stress about when I should call her, and she didn't have to wonder about when I might call.

DON'T FAKE IT

A big problem with dating is that people try to paint themselves in a certain light. They throw in some posturing to make themselves as attractive as possible, and while that makes some sense in the early going, you can't do that forever. It's exhausting and not genuine, and no one wants to base a relationship on something fake.

Start with honesty, including when you're confused. Tell your partner when you're unsure about something, and ask their opinion. If something's bothering you, talk to your partner and figure it out together. Choices like this show that you're honest, willing to work on things, and open to working together toward a solution. Be open to trying new things that might be a little off track from what you're used to, recognize that some of your own bad habits played a part in your previous relationships, but stick to what's important to you.

I think my father summed it up best when he gave a speech at my second wedding. He said, "Every great marriage is based on two simple things. First, you need to *find* the right partner. And then you need to *be* the right partner. Actually, neither of those two things is simple. But if you manage to do both of those things, you will have a marriage for the ages."

He was absolutely right. Finding the right person for you is only half of the battle. The other half comes down to working on yourself so you can be the right partner for someone else.

CHAPTER EIGHT

Beginning a New Relationship

People say, "Relationships are tough." No they're not. They're only tough when one person is working on it. That's right. Two people can move a couch real easy. One person can't move it at all.

—CHRIS ROCK

The beginning of a relationship is fraught with questions. When do you introduce your new partner to your children? How do you balance a new relationship with your responsibilities to your children? When do you talk to your new partner about your divorce?

Reconciling your past, present, and future lives can be difficult in the early going. My advice—at least at first—is to not even try. At the beginning of a relationship, maintain a compartmentalized life. When you're with your children, focus on them and stick to the custody schedule. Let your new dating interest know when you have the children and that you won't be available. Being up front about it reassures your partner while allowing you to keep parenting and dating separate.

When it *does* come time to discuss your past life with your new dating interest, do so in short clips. Many of the details of your previous marriage you'll find embarrassing and won't want to share. However, even the positive aspects aren't especially enjoyable to talk about, nor are they easy to hear. Talking too much about your ex is rarely a smart move.

If you get the urge to share how many years you were married and the reasons it didn't work out, put a more positive spin on it. Tell your new interest what went wrong, but focus on what you learned about yourself. "I learned the most important thing to me is having a close family and being with someone who is genuine, friendly, and open to new experiences." If your new dating interest shares those views, this positive reframing should be well received.

If you're tactful, these conversations will likely find their way out naturally. For instance, recently my wife and I were looking for a house, the process of which reminded me of my ex-wife, who was a real estate agent. She didn't want to pay someone else to put up open house signs, so she would ask me to run around and do it after work. I would be out there in a suit and tie after being in court all day planting open house signs or manning a posthole digger to put up a For Sale sign.

Other times, my ex would commit to hosting more than one open house at a time. Instead of partnering with another agent to sit at the second house, she insisted that I hang around the second house and greet people for three or four hours many Sundays. On one of these occasions, I was thirsty and checked the fridge for a solution. The owners had fifty different sodas in there, and I figured they surely wouldn't miss one. I grabbed a can, took a long swig, and looked down to see my phone ringing. It was my ex yelling at me, "They have cameras, and I just saw you take that soda and drink it! You're going to lose the sale for me!" Who knew the homeowners were that protective of their soda?

Out house hunting, I told my current wife these stories, and since many years had passed to allow enough space, we both had a good laugh.

As your own relationship progresses, it's okay for short stories or parts of stories to come out if you are both comfortable with it. In general, share if you're asked, but keep it focused and move on.

IS THIS ONE GOING TO WORK?

We can't predict the future. With any relationship, there's simply no way of knowing whether it's going to work. You're going to have to make a leap of faith, and you'll have to do so knowing that the odds of success aren't great. Southern California, for example, sees a 65 percent divorce rate on second marriages—in my opinion, because too many people don't put any effort into figuring out what went wrong the first time. That said, you can stack the deck in your favor by maintaining your list. Knowing which elements are important to you and which are not helps you avoid the same mistakes twice and points you toward a "happily ever after" marriage rather than a "Why do I keep making the same mistakes?" marriage.

To avoid the latter, your job is to come to terms with the negative aspects you brought to your previous marriage, change what you can about yourself, and be on the alert for any warning signs in your new relationship. I remember in my rush to get married the first time that I ignored a truckload of red flags. If I had looked closely at those warnings, I never would have gone through with it. I resolved not to make the same mistake the second time.

With many of my clients, the patterns of failed marriages often fall along gender lines. Many of the women I've worked with have married men they hoped they could change into their ideal version of a man. Equally misguided, many of the men I've worked with have married women they hope will never change. Neither perspective is right. Healthy relationships aren't built on who you want your partner to be (or remain) but rather on how comfortable you are with *who they are*.

CHANGES IN MODERN-DAY DATING

Dating practices have changed greatly in the past decade or so, at least in part due to the perception of divorce. Especially when compared to previous decades, the stigma of divorce is largely gone. It has become an accepted and sometimes expected part of our environment.

This isn't a bad development in and of itself. However, it has had some unfortunate side effects. For one, people are not as patient with their partners. Instead of putting in the effort required to maintain a healthy relationship, they look for quick answers to relieve whatever pain they're experiencing, which often leads to divorce. Such behavior is like an impulsive child throwing a fit as a tool to get their way.

Successful relationships take constant work. Tension is unavoidable, and you'll never be 100 percent aligned with your partner 100 percent of the time. There will inevitably be issues, and you need to know how to work through them or find help. Even some of my friends who have been married thirty years still run into some of the same problems as a couple married three years. They just get better at dealing with those problems.

A FINANCIAL CASE STUDY

Looking back to how Carol and I initially butted heads with our financial strategy offers an example of how efficient communication works wonders in relationships.

Before I met Carol, I spent money on what I needed without concern for the price tag. I still don't know what a cantaloupe or a loaf of bread cost. Seeing this, she worried that I didn't care about saving any money. It didn't matter that I'd been a relatively successful saver before meeting her. Understandably, all she saw was my somewhat cavalier attitude toward spending.

The therapist we were seeing for couples counseling—which I recommend all couples considering marriage do—suggested we have a weekly meeting to look at our budget and see what was happening with our money. We created a detailed budget and did, indeed, meet once per week. After five months, we learned that we both managed to stay pretty close to the budget without having to try too hard. As a result of the experiment, Carol stopped worrying I would spend all of our money, and I learned to worry about money a little more. The entire process had value from beginning to end. We may have had a point of contention, but we found a productive place in the middle.

TIPS TO MAKE YOUR RELATIONSHIP WORK

Remember that the reason you're with someone else is to have fun, be happy, and enjoy yourself. Start by focusing on things you enjoy together. The fun you have here will spill over into other parts of your life and everything you do. If you build a solid foundation of fun, fulfilling things, it makes small issues even smaller and that much more worth fixing. The more you focus on connecting with each other, the more incentivized you are to tackle issues before they become monsters.

To that end, I advise people to see a relationship or couples counselor *before* they get married. Choose an eight- or twelve-week course, commit to it, and show up to each session ready to discuss current or potential issues. Your therapist can help you negotiate issues with your new partner while you learn how to compromise and communicate your problems in a way that is neither offensive nor cause to go on the defensive. Think of couples therapy as relationship training to help you build baseline behaviors that will stop you from falling back into the old counterproductive habits that likely characterized your previous marriage.

After we had dated for about six months and were considering getting engaged, Carol and I attended about a dozen counseling sessions over the course of eight weeks. These sessions proved instrumental in helping us resolve a few lingering issues. For one, I often came home grumpy from work, still caught up in whatever ugliness I had dealt with that day. This upset Carol, who said it reminded her how her father used to behave when she was growing up. Seeing me like this made her feel bad.

She didn't want to see me have to work through that kind of ugliness every day.

When I saw it that way, I promised myself that by the time I got home I'd be done with work. To hold myself to this promise, I made it a point to unwind. I'd put the top down on the car, turn on some music, and sing along as loud as I could. Day in and day out, this did the trick without fail. I still do a version of this decompressing even now, and I've found that being intentional about letting the day's stress go makes it a lot easier to actually do so. Now, as soon as I pull up to the house, I'm ready to start my life away from work, without wasting energy being grumpy.

While I changed this behavior for my future wife, it also improved my relationship with my daughters. Now in their late teens, they've often remarked how much nicer it is living with me now than it was when they were younger. "You'd come home grumpy, and we didn't know why, but we knew to leave you alone for a while." It's a wonderful bonus to know that altering my behavior in such a seemingly small way could bring such a positive benefit to my family.

LEAVE THE COMPETITION OUT OF IT

In a recent stand-up special, *Tamborine,* comedian Chris Rock cleverly compares marriage to being in a band. In it, he explains that only one person at a time gets to sing lead vocals or play lead guitar. Sometimes that's you, and other times it's your spouse.

Whenever it's your spouse's turn to take the spotlight, your job is to provide support in the background. If that means you need to play tambourine, then you'd better play it like you mean it. Don't get grumpy and turn your back on the audience. Accept your role at that particular moment, and give it your best. Don't worry, your partner will repay the favor when it's your turn for the spotlight.

The biggest thing I learned from my first relationship to my current one is to leave competition out of it. It's too easy to get caught up in questions and trivial skirmishes such as who hurts more, who cares more, or who gave in last time. If you treat a relationship like a contest, you're missing the whole point of being close to someone else: working together.

When Carol and I started relationship counseling, the therapist quickly got frustrated and said, "Oh my God, you're like a brother and sister arguing over who gets the bigger piece of cake." The comment stuck with both of us. Neither of us wanted to be the kind of person who would argue over a piece of cake, and we definitely didn't like being seen as siblings. We agreed we were being ridiculous and resolved to focus on collaboration, not competition.

We also learned another useful rule: only one person at a time can be upset about something. When you're hurting, you look to the other person to take care of you. The problem is, they won't be in good position to do so if they're hurt too. One of you must put aside whatever is bothering you, however momentarily, so you can be supportive to your partner. It will help them get out of the bad place sooner and bring you both back to solid ground.

This noncompetitive approach to problem solving helps in other ways too. If you have a disagreement over decorations, for instance, ask yourself who it matters to more, you or your partner? When Carol and I set out to decorate our home together, all I cared was that it was nice. I didn't particularly care about the color scheme, so I asked her to narrow it down to a few choices, and then I would help her make the final selection. I wanted to support my new partner, so I didn't cut myself out of the process, but by limiting my role, I was able to let her take center stage while I offered "support on tambourine."

SHOULD I INTRODUCE MY EX TO MY NEW PARTNER?

Avoid this to the greatest extent possible. I get a lot of pushback on this from some people. Often, people think that if children are involved, your ex and your new partner have to get along.

No, they don't.

There's no reason to bring an unneeded burden into your world. First of all, your ex shouldn't have a chance to interview your new partner and decide if they're worthy. It doesn't matter what they think anyway, so there's no need to ignite a competition. Only in the direst circumstances should your ex be a conduit of information to your new partner.

What about school events for the children? People invariably bring up graduation and ask how to handle it when everyone wants to be there. It's fine if you're all at the same place at once, but you don't need to sit together and pretend you're all great friends. On back-to-school night when your children show off their creations from class, arrange with your ex to attend during different times to avoid an awkward scene. That way, you get bonus points since the children get to show off their work twice.

TELLING YOUR CHILDREN

When children are part of the mix, it's best to wait to tell them of the new person in your life until that relationship is solid and on its way to a long-term commitment. The biggest mistake people make is introducing their children to one person after another. That teaches children that it's okay to be with someone, let them go, and then start again. Children grow attached to new people in their lives relatively quickly. Exposing them to a merry-go-round of new faces will only cause unneeded trauma. If you're not sure your relationship will work out, it's unfair to expect a child to spend any energy on that person.

When it does come time to share your new relationship, be honest. Tell your children you met someone, you've been spending time together, and you really like each other. Explain there are things about that person you think the children will enjoy as well. Set up the conversation in a positive light while ensuring them that this new person will not change anything in terms of your current parenting or household dynamics. It goes a long way for children to know that someone new will be there to care for them just as you do.

I explained it to my daughters this way: "You have a mother and a great relationship with her. This is someone else I think you will like and have fun with because I have fun with her, and she will likely become someone else who cares about you." Be sure your children know they will always have alone time with you, but encourage them to look forward to new and exciting things as well. Start doing things with your new partner in simple, lighthearted, short-duration activities. It won't do any good to drop a bombshell by saying, "This is Lisa, and she's moving in tomorrow."

CHAPTER NINE

———

Blending Families

Being deeply loved by someone gives you strength, while loving someone deeply gives you courage.

—LAO-TZU

Eventually, a vibrant new relationship will reach a point when you both decide it's time to move in together or get married. It's an unforgettable time and an opportunity to create a successful home with your partner and children (possibly from both sides). You should find a variety of ways to frame new relationships, adjust to a stepparent role, and blend families. When considered with care and wisdom, any one of these approaches can help you usher in what could be a very rewarding season in your life.

To take a big-picture view, here's how this process might unfold. First, make sure you set up realistic expectations with your children before they meet your new partner.

Ease your children into it with outings you know they enjoy, building on a base of positives rather than dragging them to something they've never done before. If your children weren't rock climbers before, now isn't the best time to start. Not only should you consider an activity they're familiar with, you should also work to keep that activity short to avoid boredom and increase the likelihood things end on a positive note. Younger children especially are prone to tiring out after a while, so plan activities when they are at their best and that you know will go well.

From there, you can start to introduce your new partner into more neutral activities, such as coming over for breakfast or both of you picking the children up from school. Wait until the relationship between all of you is solid before bringing your partner into the homework scene, studying for tests, or responding when the child is upset. Once trust is established, your new partner can be a great help with these types of family dynamics.

Always remember that transitioning your new partner from stranger to trusted stepparent takes time. In this chapter, we'll discuss some of the biggest considerations as you move through this process, with tips for making sure you're considering the feelings of both your new partner and your children.

WHAT IF MY CHILDREN DON'T LIKE MY NEW PARTNER?

It's common for children to have difficulties accepting someone new in their immediate family life. Their loyalty is already tested when their parents split up, and now they're discovering that they will have to share you with someone else. Here are some tips for making these introductions go as smoothly as possible.

COMMUNICATE WITH YOUR PARTNER

Ensuring an ideal transition for your children and new partner means touching all the bases. Make sure your partner knows as much about your children as possible beforehand, including both their positive *and* negative traits. There shouldn't be any surprises. Your partner is an equal and someone who's going to work with you in most every part of your life. You need to share the wonderful things your children do, things they don't do so well, and areas where they need help so your partner is prepared.

For example, your child might be going through a phase where they disagree with almost everything you say, even if they're not truly disagreeing. Or perhaps they're in that stage where they say, "Yes, but..." to just about anything you say, always looking for an exception. If you explain this to your partner ahead of time, it can limit the frustration they experience in their interactions with the children, especially if they're new to the world of children.

COMMUNICATE WITH YOUR CHILDREN

If you've chosen your partner well, it's almost certain that, over time, your children will slowly get accustomed to your partner and eventually become quite attached. The short term is the tricky part. The children might be over the divorce but still have lingering issues. They might suspect this new person is trying to replace their mom or dad, or they have grown accustomed to having you all to themselves and are having trouble adjusting to the idea of sharing you.

Such concerns are common for children of divorce, but if you recognize that, you will likely find they're easily addressed. Here, as with much of the advice in this book, positive, proactive communication is crucial. Say something like, "This isn't a replacement parent. They're just someone new who I think you'll like if you're willing to give them a chance." Be clear about how much you enjoy spending time with your new partner and how you hope you will all be able to enjoy time together as a family too.

My children saw this process unfold in real time. Carol and I did everything together—yoga and spin class, hiking, the supermarket, you name it. We really liked being around each other, and my daughters saw this quickly. Watching us always joking and laughing together reinforced the idea that our home was a comfortable, lighthearted place to be. Remember, if you create a nice environment, others will want to share that space with you.

IT TAKES TIME

Even in the best environment, both you and your partner should remind each other to be patient. Your children might not be your partner's best friends right away, but they'll likely come around. In fact, most children are far more open to new relationships than adults are. They look for nice people wherever they go, and when they find them, they latch on.

At first, my children didn't say anything about my relationship one way or the other, though they have plenty of times since. Even recently, my oldest daughter said, "I love the way you and Carol are just so happy together. You do things together, you're lighthearted, and you joke around. You have a good time even when you're standing in line somewhere." Your children are always paying attention, and eventually, they will give you feedback on what they've seen and experienced.

FIND COMMON GROUND

When my girls learned early on that Carol owned a restaurant with her mom and sister, they were instantly intrigued and wanted to go see it right away. We went to breakfast there, and the girls met Carol's mother, who thrilled them with a tour of the kitchen and the prep line. They met some of the cooks, got to taste different foods, and quite enjoyed the adventure. With every visit, we got in the habit of walking through the kitchen, and soon the girls got to know everyone from the chefs down to the dishwashers and started to feel like they were part of this new place.

This opportunity to get them involved and feel welcomed in such a major part of Carol's life helped reinforce the positive environment we had created at home. Carol is a dynamic, interesting person, and my daughters could see that. As a result, they were able to connect with her on a new level, and their relationship grew naturally from there.

FINANCIAL SECURITY YOU CAN RELY ON

Financial concerns are another substantial element of divorce and transitioning to new families. However, the truth is that most blended families are more financially secure than single-parent families, since most have a dual income. When you're single, you're living off one income, which, combined with the challenge of taking on your share of the child-rearing, can lead to considerable financial stress, standing between you and the chance at an enriched and positive life.

It may feel like a risk blending your income with your new partner's, who may or may not have children of their own. However, the bottom line is if you're trying to create a happy life, a big part of that is a happy family. As with most things, if you set up the financial conversation in a positive light, that's the direction it will take. If you go into it with the expectation there will be problems, well, you asked for it. Overthinking it and inviting drama is a self-fulfilling prophecy.

CREATING A NEW HOMELIFE

Introducing your new spouse to your children and vice versa is sometimes a delicate balancing act. It's a difficult thing to admit as a parent, but if you've chosen a new partner and are committed to building a life with that person, you need to put them slightly above your children.

Here's why: as long as you've established a happy household, the children will adapt and be fine, but if you don't put your partner first, the relationship is doomed. Well, perhaps not doomed, but your job is to help balance the dynamics of your previous life with the dynamic you've created with your new partner, and you don't want to leave them feeling like the odd person out.

MOVING IN

One way I put Carol slightly ahead was in regard to living arrangements: I had an apartment, and she lived in a small house. We found a new house we liked and bought it together, but we decided not to all move in at the same time. For the first two weeks, Carol and I set up the new house so it would be decorated and fully stocked by the time the children got there. The first time they saw the place, it was clear they were moving in to a shared, established house. There was no confusion about whether the place was Carol's or mine. It was both of ours equally, and we were inviting my daughters to come live with us.

Soon after moving in, plan for a family meeting to discuss how everyone will live in the house. Set rules where you want them, and make boundaries clear. If you prefer that people only eat in the kitchen or dining room, now is your chance to not only make that clear, but also to reinforce the importance of your new relationship. Soon, everyday life will simply happen on its own, and the household will hum right along.

Establishing rules means holding yourself to new standards as well. In my previous marriage, my ex-wife was not an especially neat or tidy person, and I grew accustomed to that. Carol was the opposite, and her impressive neat streak forced me to improve my own habits, lest I get the dreaded "Why did you leave your stuff on the floor?" look after I failed to clean up for myself. Ultimately, the situation was a win-win. I'm much neater, the house is much cleaner, and the person I love is much happier.

ESTABLISH A PLAN AND STICK TO IT

Without a plan, you just sort of walk around in circles, occasionally getting lucky and hitting on good things. A plan can feel overly rigid and cumbersome at first, but if you take things step by step, everything will feel natural in time.

In the early days of blending your families, be sure to hold a lot of family meetings, just like the one we held when we first established our new home. Again, it may seem overly programmatic, but it's the best way to work things out. It's also an opportunity to show your children that your new partner is important. They are sitting right there next to you. Even if your partner doesn't say much at these meetings at first, chances are they will contribute more as they get comfortable. Along the way, your children will learn a new way of interacting.

I held every family meeting with Carol sitting next to me.

The first time we got together, I set the precedent. "This person is important to me, and we're forming a family. What she thinks matters to me, and I want it to matter to you as well." I encourage you to do the same. Put your hopes, dreams, and concerns out there instead of keeping them inside, where it doesn't help anyone and only torments you. That way, you've made clear to your children what you expect of them, which in turn should help everyone adapt to the situation more quickly.

DEFINE YOUR PARTNER'S ROLE

Again, the first thing you'll want to do is talk about things and get everything out in the open. This requires two conversations. First, explain to your children that you are building a new family and that their participation is crucial to that new family's success. Then, talk with your partner about what role they are comfortable with playing in your children's lives. Of course, you can never replace a parent, but that doesn't mean a new person can't also love, discipline, and bond with your children.

Especially early on, it's important to know how your partner envisions their participation. For instance, if your new partner is uncomfortable disciplining your children, then you can both agree that won't be their role until they are comfortable. If an issue comes up, it will be your job to take the reins and talk to the children. However, while you're in charge, your partner should still expect to be involved. During family meetings, for instance, everyone should sit down and discuss things as a family so that everyone is on the same page.

FIND YOUR PARTNER'S STRENGTHS

Just as it's helpful to understand the limits of your partner's participation, it's also useful to recognize their strengths. Your new partner likely has skills you don't but that may complement yours. Combining your skills is an excellent way to establish a firm foundation for building a new family.

For instance, when my daughters were in elementary school, I was the go-to parent when they needed a shoulder to cry on. They would talk to me about anything. Once they became teenagers, however, I increasingly found that I didn't know what they were talking about. While I consider myself well equipped in some sense to handle a range of interpersonal situations, the nuances of a teenage girl's emotional and social ecosystem were beyond me. As a result of my own upbringing, I was used to how boys responded to problems, often through arguments or fights that were over and forgotten by the next day. Girls, however, often carry resentment around and form alliances and cliques, and I had no idea how to relate to that.

One time in particular, my oldest daughter came home

and said she had a bad fight with her best friend. I was appalled and told her she should just forget that incident and forget that person.

"But Dad, she's my best friend," she said.

Confused, I suggested she go talk to Carol, and they went up to my daughter's room and talked for two hours. There was no solution because it wasn't a solution issue: my daughter simply had to talk out what she was feeling to someone else who'd understand. I'd been trying to protect my daughter from getting hurt, but I had been far too emotional about it. Carol understood my daughter's needs better and was able to connect as a woman in a way that I couldn't. It was a great learning moment for me, and an ideal example of the benefit of having someone else in my life I could count on to step up when sticky scenarios came along.

Carol was more than happy to be the person my daughters could talk to, and my daughters quickly bonded with her because of that. In some senses, she became less of a stepparent and more of a friend who keeps everyone comfortable. She and the girls would go off into their bedroom, talk for an hour or so, and then resolve the issue. Later, Carol would share the story with me so I could at least be apprised of the goings-on in my daughters' lives, and everyone was better off for it.

Parents are part disciplinarian, part teacher, and part friend. You have to balance those three to keep things on an even keel. The more you are tested on the dynamics you've set up for the house, the more you will need step up as a parent. This won't always be fun, but ultimately, it's part of the job.

This is all to say that setting up a new household won't be a smooth journey. You will encounter bumps and setbacks as your children find ways to test your limits. Sometimes, they will be unreasonably stubborn and committed to doing things their own way. All this stubbornness may be wasted energy and ego, but it's also part of growing up, learning what matters and what doesn't. The key is for you to remember when to put your foot down and enforce house rules.

The good news is that while your children have the capacity to be infinitely stubborn, they also have the capacity to be infinitely patient. Most children get so tired of family meetings that they will stop breaking the rules and testing limits just to avoid them. In my childhood, family meetings happened all the time, and I hated them. By the time we were halfway through elementary school, my sister and I schemed to limit those discussions as best we could. "Just don't do anything bad," one of us would say. "We're going to have to sit there for an hour, everyone will have to express their feelings, and we'll have to support each other and come to a decision. We could be outside playing. Let's just be good."

QUELLING THE ANXIETY OF BLENDED FAMILIES

Understandably, many people are nervous about blending families in one home. New environments and new personalities don't always mesh, but opportunity abounds to create a stimulating and enriching environment.

BLENDING HAS BENEFITS

If you and your new partner both have children and you find yourselves doing the *Brady Bunch* routine, you will encounter a few additional conflicts and challenges. That said, you can still follow the same basic approach of talking everything out. Sit down with everyone, figure out the rules, and encourage everyone to work together. And remember, working together means not playing favorites with just your children or spending time and doing things together in your own way at the exclusion of others.

Believe it or not, blending families often comes with adaptive benefits for your children. Psychological literature over the past twenty years shows that children of blended families are better problem solvers than those from traditional families. This research suggests that when people who haven't always lived with each other are thrown together, they make a conscious effort to get along, compromise, and work out differences—all skills that allow children to become much more effective as adults.

On the other hand, children in a traditional, married, two-parent household scenario grow up with specific ways of doing things, don't have too much input, and don't develop elevated negotiating skills. Findings like this reinforce the idea that the more people around that care about your children, the better—whether it's mom, dad, grandparents, cousins, or a new stepmom or stepdad. Each can add positive reinforcement in your children's daily lives.

BUILD A COHESIVE FAMILY

Keeping your space or dividing the family into cliques is the best way to sabotage that future. The biggest mistake I see people make when blending families is still doing things with their children separate from the rest of the family. Naturally, you will have a greater fondness for your children. They are *yours*, after all, and you know them much better than your new stepchildren. No one's expecting you to immediately have the same fondness for your partner's children as you do for your own.

However, to make this transitional period run smoother,

it's important that you don't play favorites. Instead of going bowling with just you and your children on Thursday nights, make it an open invitation. Show the new members of your family that they are just as important. Do as much together as possible. I have seen many families where both partners came in with their own children, and they never managed to blend the two groups together. Each partner would take their respective children on separate spring breaks and then later take their own vacation as a couple, but never as a whole family. That doesn't give your children *or* your partner any sense of togetherness, and it may serve to drive the new family apart over time.

This is not to say that there is never an opportunity for alone time with your children, or for your new partner to spend alone time with their children, for that matter. Alone time matters and should be pursued at appropriate times. However, just make sure that these little moments don't encroach on too much of your family time. If they do, this continued division of the family will override any of the benefits of having a blended family.

ESTABLISH COMFORTABLE PHYSICAL SPACE

When both you and your new partner are bringing children into the equation, there's usually no getting around it: you're going to need a bigger house. But how big?

Should your new blended family be expected to share rooms, or should they each get their own?

If resources allow, my advice is generally to follow whatever precedent has already been set. If all of the children involved previously had their own rooms, they shouldn't be expected to start sharing rooms now. Especially in the early going, there is great value to everyone having their own space. Remember, your children are learning to navigate new relationships with new people. There's no sense in putting even more pressure on those children by shoving them into the same room with someone, especially with a potential new stepsibling. We all need a place where we can retreat, decompress, and recover.

ADDING MORE CHILDREN TO THE FAMILY

At some point in your new relationship, you might decide to have more children, which of course brings new challenges. Especially if the children in your blended family are already a little older, adding an infant to the mix invites the potential of them feeling there's not enough love to go around. So before you add any new children, take some time to assure your older children that there is always enough love.

The truth is, even as parents, we need occasional reminders that our capacity for love is limitless. Before my second daughter was born, I worried constantly that I wouldn't love her as much as I loved my first. However, from the first time I held her, I found myself bonding with her just as deeply, and soon we had our own routines and games that were different from those I shared with my first child but no less important. As a psychologist, I understood this would likely be the case. But as a sometimes irrational human being, I still worried that I wouldn't be as close with my new child. I've never been happier to be so wrong.

Reassure your children that you understand their concerns, and share your own experiences with similar struggles if you ever had them. Assure them that as soon as their new sibling arrives, all those worries will go right out of their heads. Yes, life schedules and activities will need to be rearranged, but your love and their own will quickly expand to this new member of the family. Your children may doubt you as you explain all this, but when they see it in action, they'll soon become believers. New babies get lots of attention, for sure, and the older children will continue to receive it as well, just in different ways than they are used to.

As much as they are interested, include your children in baby activities, such as helping with a bath, feeding, or even changing diapers. This reinforces your goals of togetherness and helps your children bond more quickly with their new sibling. My daughters were in high school when Carol and I had our son, so they were old enough not to worry that I wouldn't love them as much. Babies are cute, cuddly, and funny, and both my girls were thrilled to have a baby brother and jumped right in to help.

If you want to make the most of this second chance and build a new family that is truly happy and connected, you have to put all of your energy into it. It doesn't happen by itself. The more you bring to your role as both a partner and a parent, the more that love and care will trickle down into the rest of the family.

Be careful, however, because the inverse is also true. When things aren't going your way and you're unhappy, your family picks up on that too and becomes unhappy right along with you. Always remember that a successful second chance starts with you, what kind of family you want to have, and how you want to treat each other.

To take care of everyone else, you must always remember to first take care of yourself. It's a lot of work balancing a new spouse, children, possibly a new child, and a career. Maintain focus on what makes *you* happy as opposed to just brightening everyone else's day. This is tough for some people. They try too hard to please others and end up neglecting themselves. You are the center of what you created. The stronger that center is, the stronger your family will be as a whole.

Conclusion

SETTING SAIL

Twenty years from now, you will be more disappointed by the things you didn't do than those you did. So throw off the bowlines. Sail away from safe harbor. Catch the wind in your sails. Explore. Dream. Discover.

—MARK TWAIN

After a divorce, you have a second chance to redesign your life in every aspect. You can adjust your mental and emotional functions, financial strategies, where to live, who your friends are, and the way you see your family. Look at each of these and decide what works and what doesn't work, keeping in mind that only partly working *isn't good enough*. It's either working or it's not, and it can always be improved.

Often, this process of auditing your life means making some tough choices. You'll likely find yourself parting with many habits, possessions, and people other than your ex-spouse. As you ask yourself whether you want something in your life or not, just remember that as you abandon the people and things that no longer serve a purpose, you're replacing them with people and things that *do*.

With each area of your life, keep a laser-sharp focus on identifying problems, and be sure to call them what they are—problems—because if you don't label them as such, you won't feel compelled to fix them. Once you identify a problem, generate as many solutions as possible and write them all down, with no caveats, self-doubt, or second-guessing. Keep everything nice and systematic. Look at each potential solution and decide, "If I did this, what would it lead to?" When you complete that process for your entire list, you'll have one or two clear winning solutions for every problem. That's basic "problem solving" and the best way to tackle any problems you may encounter.

At that point, jump in and try the solution. Many people spend way too much time thinking and rethinking about what they should do, but if you just follow the steps, the best solution will rise to the top. Besides, if it turns out you chose the wrong solution and it didn't solve the problem, remember, it's not a tragedy. At least you were being proactive and moving your life forward. Whenever these occasional missteps occur, just take a half step back, reassess where you are, and try again. Your next choice will likely be more successful.

Barbara Bush, former First Lady of the United States, was the commencement speaker at my graduation from the University of Pennsylvania in 1990. I only recall two things from her twenty-minute speech that she told the graduating class. First, she said that she doubted anyone would remember what she was telling us in twenty years' time. Second, she said something to the effect of, and I'm paraphrasing, "You are standing at the edge of the dock that your education has taken you to. It's time to set sail!"

I always loved that saying—so much so that I tried to get the transcript of her speech to share with you at the end of this book. Unfortunately, all roads to progress in this endeavor led to dead ends. Mrs. Bush's speech was delivered in the pre-YouTube days, so it wasn't online. I searched the University of Pennsylvania archives too. Still nothing. Finally, I posted to the Class of 1990 Penn Facebook page to see if anyone maybe had some old video of it. I got all sorts of amazing suggestions from my classmates (email the speechwriter, check the George H. W. Bush archives, etc.), none of which panned out. All of my classmates who responded, including one who admitted taking forty-five minutes to search for the speech online rather than doing what she was supposed to be doing at work, remembered that Mrs. Bush had said that nobody would remember her speech, and that she said something about "setting sail."

Ultimately, that's good enough. Just like you don't need to know the exact details of Mrs. Bush's speech, you don't need to know every stop on your journey in order to set sail. If you're standing on the dock worrying about what's ahead—about bad weather, rough seas, or breaking the rudder—you'll never cast off, you'll never explore, you'll never discover how wide and wonderful the ocean truly is. By now, you've experienced a lot of life and learned a thing or two about how to make it work. Now it's time to take those lessons, get in the boat, and go. Sure, the journey won't always be a smooth one, but be confident that you are fully capable of finding solutions. It's better to be out there sailing than tied to the dock.

I wrote this book based not only on my professional life, but also on the things I got right—and the many I got wrong—following my own divorce. My hope is you can learn from my own experience so that you can skip as much of the bad stuff as possible and hit the ground running with your own second chance.

Now, it's your turn to set sail. May the wind always be at your back.

Acknowledgments

First, I'd like to thank my amazing wife, Carol, for her overwhelming love, encouragement, and support as I worked through the writing and editing of this book. I have found that I can do many good things on my own, but the best things come when I get Carol involved.

Next, I need to thank my writing coach, Chas Hoppe, and my publisher, Katherine Sears, for the kind, consistent, and always positive encouragement they gave me at every step during the outlining, writing, editing, and publishing of my first book. You helped make what, at first, seemed like an insurmountable obstacle into a series of easily achieved stages.

I have to thank my college roommate and best friend, Jeffrey Hyman, for giving me the idea to write this book, for helping me find my publishing team, for giving me endless ideas for marketing the book, and for reviewing numerous versions of the text. Jeffrey is the ultimate entrepreneur, and a little bit of his business sense has finally rubbed off on me.

I need to thank the co-shareholders of my law firm, Enenstein Pham & Glass, for their patience and continued support of this past year as I've set aside most of my administrative duties at the firm to write this book.

I'd also like to thank the over five hundred clients I've worked with since 1997, when I turned from clinical psychology to family law. In the early years, you taught me what it meant to be both empathetic and empowering at the same time. In the later years, you allowed me to help you with a broader scope of your lives beyond the basics of divorce. Your stories populate my practice and now this book.

Finally, I must thank my parents, Harry and Eileen Glass. You've done so much for me, from setting up a college fund that kept me debt free, despite my overeducation, to helping me choose my first house to helping me decide to start my first solo practice and to always being a source of love and support. But, perhaps, the most important thing you showed me, through your own actions, was that by consistent, hard work with a steadfast partner by your side, anything is possible.

About the Author

 When author **DAVID J. GLASS** went through his own divorce over a decade ago, he was surprised at how few resources were available to help guide him through the year that came after the divorce was finalized. Drawing from his own post-divorce journey, as well as from over two decades of experience—first as a therapist and currently as a family law attorney—David wrote *Moving On* to help others pick themselves up, set a new course, and start moving forward.

With dual training in psychology and law, David has helped guide hundreds of clients through the often confusing landscape of life after divorce. In that time, he has also taught various psychology and law classes in both undergraduate and graduate settings, worked as the associate editor for the *Los Angeles Psychologist*, and become a regular contributor for publications such as *Divorce* and *Hitched*. As a commentator and divorce expert, David has appeared on national programs such as *Extra*, and local TV and radio programs such as Fox's *Good Day LA* and KABC Radio, and he has been quoted in publications such as the *New York Daily News*, *People*, and the *Huffington Post*.

More recently, he joined the board of the Alzheimer's Association, where he uses his position to help raise awareness and advocate for a disease that is underdiagnosed and underfunded. He is also a certified pastor who can perform marriages, though he is still waiting to marry his first couple.

David lives in Los Angeles, California, with his wife, Carol, a restaurateur who runs the Catering and Special Events Department at Joan's on Third, her family's business. Along with their two-year-old son and his two adult daughters from his previous marriage, David and his family can usually be found out and about enjoying a variety of activities under the Southern California sun.